WESTERN MOVIES

WESTERN

The Movie Treasury

MOVIES

The Story of the West on Screen

Walter C. Clapham

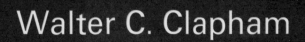

Galley Press

Introduction

Imagine for a moment a whole month's festival of superlative Western movies screened in those Happy Hunting Grounds to which all keen film-goers with a weakness for Westerns hope to be safely gathered in.

Which pictures would you choose—if the Heavenly Selection Committee were prepared to listen to your choice?

It's a fascinating thought and it occurred to me after I had seen *The Gunfighter* for the fourth time. I voiced it aloud that evening and around the fire we took it from there. Which films would we put alongside *The Gunfighter* (all of us agreed on that one) in our great indulgent celestial movie show?

Out came ballpoints and scruffy bits of paper and from that moment on this book began.

No two lists of 'musts' agreed. Very few lists will agree when *you* play the game. There will, however, be a good deal of common ground and the purpose of this book is to provoke discussion about this area—to examine Westerns of high entertainment and artistic merit, not in an obsessive way, but rather from the standpoint of the film-goer of catholic tastes who is interested in all forms of cinema and, indeed, in matching the best of each and every form.

A book, also, about the making of Westerns, the people who make them, and the whole historical backcloth to the Western film, a knowledge of which I personally consider essential to its true understanding, and, anyway, vastly exciting.

My opinions will, of course, be challenged—it was ever thus on the Western movie battlefront—but they do, at least, come from long appreciation. It started at the age of four in a tin hut when Tom Mix on a dim and flickering screen reined back his horse Tony with such élan and such a flash of daunting teeth and hooves that the whole place rocked.

The retired schoolmarm, eking out her paltry pension with 'boots and saddle' thumpings on the piano, was stricken by temporary paralysis. My last memory of her before plunging in my excitement from the backless bench was of her one hand frozen over the keys and the other clutching at her skimpy bosom.

As for me, I was lost amid a sea of hobnailed boots, no less daunting than the hooves, until rescued by my irate cousin Elsie. Short of temper and heavy of hand was Elsie.

The experience changed my life, coloured it enormously through the formative years. My tastes have altered but my affection abides. It still seems to me that there is a kind of magic in the harmonious movement of a man and a horse and in words like sagebrush, sierra and mesquite.

NOTE *The dates of films given throughout this book are approximate. This is because of varying lengths of production-period, the intervals between production and distribution and differing dates of distribution in various territories. In most cases the date given is the year of principal production.*

Contents

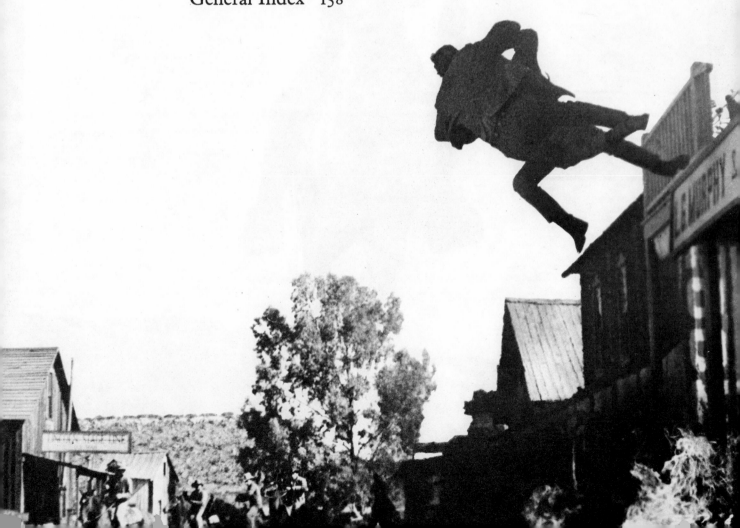

Why the Western?

'THE WESTERN,' James Stewart once observed with pride, 'is an original. An American feels "this is ours!"'

In these few words a man who has contributed much to the Western film put his trigger-finger unerringly on the main source of its appeal. At its best it is imbued with a feeling of one nation's history communicated by players and directors who have a vested national interest in the theme. They may feel pride or misgiving, they may have a mixture of feelings, but they are concerned.

It is this concern that is communicated to the audience. And it doesn't matter that truth has become heavily encrusted with legend. At the back of it all there's a grain of truth and this is what is being interpreted. The audience goes home pondering: 'Was it something like this?' and the 'it'

exerts a never-failing fascination—less than 30 years of highly compressed, turbulent history, unique in its sweep and tensions, and the bizarre backcloth against which it was played.

The backcloth gives it its potency. Successful scenes from a Western that aims high—even though it may fall by the wayside—ensure that it is never entirely forgotten. The opening sequences of *The Big Country* (1958) with that high, wide and handsome buggy ride, open up a whole visual concept of Texas as never realized before. If one were compiling an anthology of impact-making opening sequences, then *The Big Country* would surely be included, as, incidentally, would John Huston's *Moulin Rouge* (1955), a film in another genre that also promised much and broke the promise.

Gregory Peck (left) and Charlton Heston (right) starred in The Big Country *(Anthony-Worldwide 1958), a Western that started well but ran out of steam.*

LEFT *Joel McCrea, a Western stalwart, with Maureen O'Hara in* Buffalo Bill *(20th Century Fox 1944)*. RIGHT *James Stewart up against one of 'the baddies' in* Firecreek *(WB/ Seven Arts 1967)*. OVERLEAF *A battle scene from Ralph Nelson's horrific* Soldier Blue *(Avco-Embassy 1970), a film that dealt with the Westerners' inhumanity to their 'red brothers'.*

When a Western aims high and succeeds completely it leaves behind a whole legacy of scenes that seem printed on the eyeball. When the naïve and brashly brave Elisha Cook Jun. challenges the arch-professional Jack Palance in *Shane* (1953) and dies, he is so palpably, terribly dead that the moment is imperishable. How often the mind returns to and lingers on the domestic scenes in *Shane*—Van Heflin, Jean Arthur, Alan Ladd and Brandon De Wilde, transfixed in the humble cabin like subjects in Dutch painting interiors.

It could be argued that once the movie-camera had been invented the Western was well-nigh inevitable. Once the camera was in the hands of a nation whose creed was mass-production, and among whose talented immigrants were a number, highly gifted in nosing out mass-market trends and needs, it could only be a matter of time before eyes looked westwards.

A great new medium of mass entertainment beckoned invitingly. But the invitation was also daunting. In terms of pure production, in terms particularly of mass production, it was also a maw that had to be constantly fed and satisfied.

Stories and situations involving movement and action—this was the demand of the newly-born camera. Where to find them?

This didn't really require any vast leap of the imagination for the trails had already been blazed. The dime novel writers had opened up the West and in no time at all had created a whole new mythology out of the Western frontier story and notably a few highly-coloured characters. The younger generation, and hosts, too, of the perennially young at heart, had new romantic names to conjure with—Buffalo Bill Cody, Wild Bill Hickok, 'Calamity Jane' Cannaray. In the week by week issue of the Western 'libraries' their deeds and experiences would have confounded Hercules himself. This kind of conveyor belt Western fiction had been started almost simultaneously with the frontier situation.

LEFT *Clint Eastwood in* 2 Mules for Sister Sarah *(Universal/Malpaso 1969).*
ABOVE Buffalo Bill *(20th Century Fox 1944) was about a frontiersman, who finished up touring the world with his own Wild West Show.*

In some ways the dime novel writers and their publishers could be likened to today's pop group promoters. The prime case is of William Cody, who was certainly a buffalo hunter, Indian scout and frontiersman of some considerable repute, but was nevertheless 'discovered' and transformed into the hero of a serial in a New York publication.

From then on success bred success and no doubt the recounting of partially true experiences bred a multitude of others for which the kindest word is legendary. As far as William (Buffalo Bill) Cody was concerned he struck it rich in the West in a way that he would probably never have done had he tried his luck in Nevada or the Black Hills of Dakota, or wherever the prospect of gold was timely and convenient. He exploited the West in much the same way that he himself had been initially exploited. He formed his own Wild West Show and

toured the world with it for much of a highly profitable lifetime.

The early film producers therefore knew that they had a ready-made and popular theme right on their doorsteps. Whatever qualms they might have—if they had time or concern for them right at the beginning—about there being only so many permutations of plot and situation, these qualms were to be dispelled later when they found that Western fans, far from being affronted by predictability, actually seemed to appreciate it. In other words, the Western took on the ritual element that has never forsaken it, best expressed, perhaps, in its duellist-gunfighter ingredient.

The climactic set-piece of this law-and-order brand of Western is as predictable as it is in a bullfight. The afficianado likes it this way! All depends on interpretation and style.

ABOVE *George Barnes in* The Great Train Robbery *(Edison 1903)*.
BELOW RIGHT *A scene from this trail-blazing Western.*
ABOVE RIGHT *Dustin Farnum (*right*) in another early Western* The Squaw
Man *(Jesse L. Lasky Feature Co. 1913)*.

Keystone of the whole extraordinary edifice was an Edison Films production—*The Great Train Robbery*—made in 1903. Directed by Edwin S. Porter, and shot in New Jersey, it can fairly claim the honour, since it was obviously based on the none too distant exploits of Western train robbers such as Jesse James and the Wild Bunch. Murder on the Express, a chase on horseback, an ultimate gunfight 'twixt goodies and baddies . . . here was the original outlaw picture.

From then on, the assembly line, as it were, got under way. . . .

An entirely new character, or romantic image, came into the lives of millions, and captured many of them for keeps.

This was the 'cowboy', who was based on the hard-working drovers who herded longhorns from Texas to the Kansas railheads and later became the ranching cowhands. It was only a brief period of glory but the cowboy has long outlived the actuality.

As he appeared to cinema audiences he was not only cattle-drover, rounder-upper of strays and horseman-virtuoso. He was also a sort of latter-day Sir Galahad, righter of wrongs and general expression of a new sort of derring do, with his spurs and chaps and ten-gallon hat.

Audiences saw him personified through the years by a gallery of stars who played nothing but cowboys' parts. Each star was, in fact, The Cowboy to the faithful fans, whose loyalty was unquestioning and never particularly demanding. It was enough that he should come riding once more through sagebrush on a familiar starry horse—a cue for hard-pressed cinema pianists to extemporize boot and saddle themes.

First of a long line was Broncho Billy Anderson, who had already appeared in *The Great Train Robbery*. Anderson, whose real name was Max Aronson, was a chunky former vaudeville actor who had never really made it on the stage. The Broncho Billy character emerged in a 1908 one-reeler and proved immensely popular. Thereafter Anderson worked his lucky seam through eight years and some 400 films. He could truthfully claim that he was the first real 'star' in a great industry that would make much of the word. Hefty, intrinsically likeable, competent enough for the simple requirements of his films, he presented to audiences a character that they found immensely sympathetic and wanted to see again and again. Max, for his part, saw that they did.

The Western was in at the very birth of Hollywood. In 1913 three remarkable men set off for what was to become the film capital of the world. They were Samuel Goldfish, a glove salesman, later to be known as Samuel Goldwyn, Jesse Lasky, a vaudeville producer, and Cecil B. DeMille, a former playwright and actor. They went as partners and their first project was a film version of the Broadway success, *The Squaw Man*, starring Dustin Farnum.

It was inevitable that Anderson would have a successor. In fact, there were two, whose careers ran almost simultaneously. In their different ways they probably spell 'cowboy star' more than any other actors who have concentrated entirely on Westerns. The illustrious names are W. S. Hart and Tom Mix.

Hart was born in the West, loved it and its traditions, and was a stickler for accuracy when it came to Western detail. His work therefore had both integrity and realism. It was also endowed with a certain poetic quality that earned and still earns respect. He took his Westerns extremely seriously—perhaps a little too seriously for the circumstances of his time. Judged in a broader concept, he was a technical initiator since, in his favoured strong, silent persona, he gave us the first experience of what we now call dead-pan acting.

Tom Mix couldn't match him either for acting experience or ability—Hart had come to films from the stage—but the former horse-wrangler and rodeo rider certainly had the edge when it came to riding ability. It was his stunts and horsemanship—and, perhaps, especially his rapport with his horse Tony, as showy a performer as he was—that made him into the most financially successful of all genuine one-track cowboy stars.

Mix could hardly have been called a plastic cowboy when his physical skills were so apparent, yet what he stood for, and what the others stood for, who followed his particular trail, smelt of the assembly line, a mechanical, gimmicky catering for a mass market. It would be churlish to deny that he meant much to millions, particularly youngsters, in the early nineteen-twenties, but it would also be unrealistic not to admit that his formula was largely responsible for the failure of the Western to rise from the dumps in the thirties. Certainly Mix never pointed the way to a Western of real stature, something in concept and execution that would put it on terms with more ambitious cinema.

That attempt was to be made in 1923, when the world duly sat up and took notice of James Cruze's *The Covered Wagon*, which starred J. Warren Kerrigan and Lois Wilson, although it would hardly figure now in anyone's list—however personal—of great Westerns. Still, it was a big deal in all ways. It was conceived in 'epic' style—a spectacular story of early pioneering—and this is important in itself. It's a milestone movie despite its imperfections. You can pick holes in it, mainly because of its plotting. W. S. Hart, speaking as Western 'authority', found other holes to pick. His meticulous mind was appalled by the sight of a wagon train camping in a vulnerable canyon and of cattle trying to cross a river while handicapped by neck yokes. He said they were 'errors that would make a Western man refuse to speak to his own brother'.

But it had cost over 750,000 dollars, which showed an awful amount of faith for those days in a Western and it justified this faith by grossing about 4,000,000 dollars.

Following hard on the heels of *The Covered Wagon* came *The Iron Horse* (1924), which was the work of a young director whose name, above all, was to be associated with the classic Western. John Ford was already a well-established Western director by the time he came to this pioneering railroad epic. Westerns were to return to this theme again and again, acknowledging the role that railways had played in opening up the West.

There had been typically bizarre and flamboyant touches to the building of these railways. Union Pacific had been given the charter to go westwards and the Central Pacific company was similarly chartered to head east from California. The old saying that the eastern portion of the track was built on booze and the western on tea is, in fact, another way of admitting that it was Irish and imported Chinese labour that made the whole project possible.

It was an epic enterprise, deserving of the epic treatment that some films were to give it. Desert, snows, Indians and constant toil (four rails were laid a minute) was the lot of the labourers. For weekend relaxation there were mobile brothels, gambling hells and dance halls.

Work was started in 1863. The Civil War naturally delayed it, but in May, 1869, the two tracks neared at Promontory Point in Utah. On May 10 a gang of Chinese put the final Central Pacific rail into place and a gang of specially spruced-up Irishmen performed the same task on behalf of Union Pacific. Ceremonial spikes were driven in, the champagne flowed, and directly the news was telegraphed throughout the nation cannons were fired on the shores of both oceans and cities celebrated in a variety of ways. Chicago held a procession seven miles long.

It was altogether an extravagant celebration but not really out of keeping with the importance of what had been achieved. Years had been pared from the laborious business of opening up the West.

'Epic' is possibly an understatement for Ford's vast treatment of the railroad theme in *The Iron Horse*.

BELOW *A scene from the early railroad epic* The Iron Horse *(Fox 1924).*
LEFT *John Ford, the director, with his camera crew.*

ABOVE *John Wayne, the 'daddy' of all Western movie stars, in his first starring rôle in* The Big Trail *(Fox 1930).*
BELOW *The amorous serenader here is Warner Baxter; the film* In Old Arizona *(Fox 1929).*
RIGHT *Richard Dix starred in* Cimarron *(RKO 1931), a highly ranked film of its time.*

He had already directed 35 features and perhaps a dozen two-reelers at this point of his career so perhaps he thought it was time for some sort of celebration of his own. It became the longest film in his whole history of film-making (two hours and forty minutes). And if we are to trust his version of what happened, it was another case of Little Topsy who just 'grew and grew and grew'.

He obviously had a soft spot for it and (with his tongue in his cheek?) he did say that it was a simple little story that somehow turned into a 'so-called epic', as if he were surprised by it all.

More and more money was spent on it and the result was Fox's biggest ever production. It is almost certain that this was never the intention at the outset. It was shot, largely on location, in Nevada, and the working conditions were tough for the big cast, if not quite as tough as for 'the Paddies and Chinks' who had actually built the railway. It was 20° below zero when the cast assembled, which wasn't funny, since some of them, Ford has said, were still wearing summer clothes.

George O'Brien, a former stunt man, was the star. O'Brien was to have a distinguished career as a player and director in Westerns.

It was Ford's more fluid techniques for handling the Indian battle scenes—set-pieces in both films—that gave *The Iron Horse* a much greater distinction than *The Covered Wagon*. Plus, of course, the kind of editing that is the hallmark of real talent.

Here was action that had its own rhythms so that the audience couldn't help but be involved. In essence it proclaimed what cinema of this sort is all about. It is certainly, in the context of great Westerns, a film of more importance than *The Covered Wagon* although this was more acclaimed at the time.

The Big Trail (1930) was to be the next truly memorable Western, staged in epic style. It made a star out of John Wayne, an early protégé of Ford, although it was Raoul Walsh who directed this picture.

With the coming of sound the Western had dithered nervously as indeed had other brands of films during a time when movement all but went out of the movies. There *were* technical difficulties —not the least of them the fact that the camera's own noise had to be eliminated and that the boom (for the microphone) hadn't yet put in an appearance.

But although Walsh's *In Old Arizona* (1929) was no masterpiece, it did prove that sound troubles could be overcome, and that sound in fact might even enhance the Western. Walsh hammered home the point in *The Big Trail*—in which wagons westwards was the theme again. This early sound Western is still visually a most impressive piece of work. There are scenes here that confirm the 'printed on the eyeball' concept—wagons trying to ford a storm-swollen river; and the usual set-piece of Indians circling a wagon-train turned in on its tail, like a caterpillar, probably never better done. The plot, in human terms, was undistinguished, but as spectacle this was one for the honours list.

An honourable mention, too, for *Cimarron* (1931), at least for its opening portion which was the truly Western part of it. Directed by Wesley Ruggles this is primarily the story of the founding of a state.

The state was to be Oklahoma, but on the morning of April 22, 1889, it was a huge piece of land, about two million acres, lying between Indian reservations, occupied by 22 Indian tribes.

Land-hungry settlers had long demanded that it should be opened up, and finally Presidential permission was given to open part of it. At noon, troops stationed on the borders would fire their guns into the air and blow their bugles and there would begin one of the most desperate, confused land-rushes of all time—desperate simply because it was obvious then that Western land was running out, certainly the land of cheap government grants.

Lining the borders were the prospective settlers on horseback, in buggies, in prairie schooners and on foot. When the guns fired and the bugles blew here was spectacle—a vision of ultimate pioneering —and it was in conveying the mood and the sweep of this extraordinary land-race, that *Cimarron* triumphed.

Starring Richard Dix, an actor of improbable larger-than-life masculinity, pointed by a jaw that jutted like a jetty, and the ever-gracious Irene Dunne, *Cimarron* soon strayed from purest Western trails as characterization took over more and more from the visual element. But there was no doubt about its impact at the time.

Looking back, one would have thought that enough good spadework had been done to ensure a prospect of full-blown, quality-conscious Westerns in the thirties, but it didn't happen this way. It was a lean period with the producers concentrating 'full-length' resources and ambitions on other fields. There were the musicals, taking in a complete range that could happily accommodate emotive backstage as in *Forty Second Street* (1933), extravaganzas such as those starring Eddie Cantor, the burgeoning and now embarrassing choreography of Busby Berkeley, and the sophisticated and mostly delightful story-with-music vehicles of Astaire and Rogers.

There were gangster films, biographies, dramas with social comment and dramas without them. And, of course, a delicate crop of sophisticated comedies. But Westerns that would appeal to an ever larger and increasingly sophisticated audience were few and far between. The truth of it was that they were rather small beer in the thirties. Denigrating terms were to enter the language—'horse operas', 'sage-brushers'.

This is not to say that they weren't there and that there was not a huge faithful public for them. But the Western now was determinedly riding a somewhat blinkered trail—the one that had been basically blazed by Mix.

Mix had set the pattern for other stars—Buck Jones, Ken Maynard, Tim McCoy, Hoot Gibson—who did series of pictures, and it is casting no real aspersion on their efforts to say that among their multitude of fans were serried ranks and ranks of idolizing children.

And there were serials, of course (they had always been popular), but the thirties, essentially, provided the heyday of the 'B' Western, although, in fact, it was to linger on until after the Second World War.

It was a conveyor belt Western, often skimping on sets and locations, plumping most often for the stereotyped, giving and demanding little in the way of imagination. But the fans wouldn't have had it otherwise. There were implications of cult elements in the whole phenomenon—the furnishing of a fantasy life. This sort of fan would probably hold that it was the 'true' Western and wouldn't give a thank-you for your so-called 'epic', 'classic' or 'adult' Western, whatever you cared to call it.

It flourished and some astonishing hybrids were to spring from it.

In 1935 the first Hopalong Cassidy film was made—it was based on the Clarence E. Mulford books—and this was to develop into one of the most popular Western series of all time. William Boyd, although no horseman at the outset, learned fast and in Hopalong created a character not without a touch of originality and some charm. It saw him through some seventy adventures. The tail-enders never matched his mid-period, but television was to give the character a new lease of life.

Perhaps even more remarkable was the rise of the Singing Cowboys, considered by connoisseurs as the most regrettable lapse in the history of the genre. But again, their popularity at the time was enormous.

They began chirruping first in the form and larynx of Gene Autry in the same year as the Cassidy debut. It was Autry's films, in particular, that seemed to cock a snook at all tradition when they developed into a format of modern backgrounds. But they were slickly done and never really matched by the vehicles of the Autry successors, such as Tex Ritter, Dick Foran, Bob Baker and Roy Rogers who in the early forties came closest to matching Autry's popularity.

No glimmer in the Western sky of bigger and better things?

There were efforts with more ambition. Cecil B. DeMille, arch apostle of spectacle, obviously decided to seek it in the West, as a sort of afterthought, and his own offering was *The Plainsman* (1936). Ballyhoo attended it at the time and it is still by no means unentertaining although you can't help but note that it creaks on occasions with staginess. DeMille had a production-minded man's commitment to studio sets. There is also an air of contrivance about the surely improbable get-

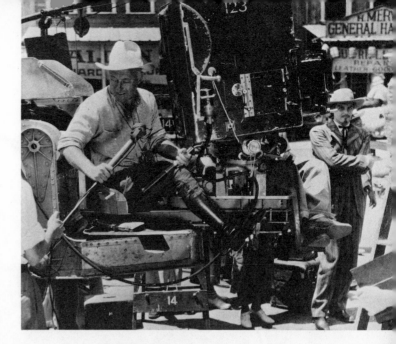

LEFT *Perhaps the most extraordinary phenomenon was the 'Hopalong Cassidy Cult'.*
ABOVE *Cecil B. DeMille found fresh opportunities for spectacle in* The Plainsman *(Paramount 1936). One of the stars was Jean Arthur (below), who played the frontier hellcat, Calamity Jane.*

together of Western notorieties. Involved in this great Round Up of favourite Western characters are: Buffalo Bill (James Ellison), Wild Bill Hickok (Gary Cooper), Calamity Jane (Jean Arthur), glamorised beyond all recognition of the hard-bitten original, and Jack McCall (Porter Hall).

Even our old friend General Custer (John Miljan) has managed to make it.

There is some good minor playing by Charles Bickford and Porter Hall but, as always, it is Cooper who stands out. It was evident very early

ABOVE *and* BELOW *Two scenes from* Wells Fargo *(Paramount 1937) starring Joel McCrea, which glorified an early Western means of communication.*
TOP RIGHT *Walter Brennan and Gary Cooper in* The Westerner *(Sam Goldwyn 1940).*
BELOW RIGHT *A typical rip-roaring scene from* Union Pacific *(Paramount 1939).*

on that here was someone who couldn't help but grace a Western. His early fortunes had been founded in Henry King's silent Western *The Winning of Barbara Worth* (1926). Cooper had also been impressive in the first sound version of *The Virginian* (1929). Bill Hart's strong and so silent persona had been passed on and was now in good hands. Cooper always looked as if he'd been born to wear buckskin.

Wells Fargo (1937) starring Joel McCrea heading a cast that included Bob Burns, Francis Dee, Lloyd Nolan and John Mack Brown, was a long transportation epic (how long it seemed!) whose wheels never really got out of a rut despite McCrea's presence. He was another natural Westerner who was to dedicate most of his career to such roles.

DeMille returned with *Union Pacific* (1939) which followed the tracks pioneered by *The Iron Horse*. DeMille's rail-roading epic owed a debt or two to Ford. He was obviously influenced by *The Iron Horse* and there *are* some sequences which seem more than derivative—in fact, they are remarkably similar. But it was a film that nevertheless deserved the warm reception that it got.

Here was Joel McCrea again, this time in fine form with something more worthy of his talents. McCrea played a trouble-shooter whose task was to keep the transcontinental project moving. Barbara Stanwyck played opposite as the fiery Irish postmistress of the mobile railway town.

Miss Stanwyck stage-Irished it up a bit, but a little overstatement didn't really come amiss in an all-out action mixture that took in rowdy railroad workers, turbulent frontier types of both sexes, con men, outlaws and a generous helping of Indians.

Neither did Mr. DeMille stint himself with his props—six locomotives and fifty-five cars, all of correct vintage.

Union Pacific was undoubtedly great fun although perhaps embarrassingly patriotic. But, in perspective, it is dwarfed by another film which appeared the same year and which had a profound and far-reaching influence on the course of Westerns.

John Ford had returned to the form after 13 years abstinence. John Wayne, who had been languishing in 'B' Westerns since making *The Big Trail*, was back once more in a main feature starring role.

The film was the immortal *Stagecoach* (1939) which was to set all sorts of standards for Westerns to be. In several ways it could be looked upon as a 'Now, follow that!' Western. It says much for its stature that, despite the many films that accepted the challenge, not so many have matched or excelled it.

More scenes from the action-packed Union Pacific *(Paramount 1939), starring Joel McCrea and Barbara Stanwyck.*

Go West, Young Man!

STAGECOACH bulged with *all* the required ingredients of the classic Western. It carried a full complement of the historic-pioneering elements and it also made room for that other constituent, the domestic law and order issue.

Westerns, on the whole, take two main trails. The first is essentially pioneering in the truly historic sense. It covers the journey West, the hazards of early settlement, clashes with the Indians, thinly spread protection in the form of the colourful cavalry, tenuous lines of communication (the stage-coach and the Pony Express), important historic movements such as the spectacular cattle drives north.

The second is domestic in the sense that it concerns 'family' troubles of the settlers' own making, their squabbles and their efforts to build a civilized society. The kind of film, in fact, whose ultimate classic confrontation is between gunman, outlaw and sheriff.

The two trails tend to touch at times but most memorable films do keep on track.

LEFT *'Home On The Range' was always a tougher tune than 'Home Sweet Home'*.
BELOW *John Wayne as the rumbustious Ringo Kid in John Ford's classic,* Stagecoach *(Wanger/UA 1939)*.

ABOVE *John Wayne's rifle 'speaks true' again. Another scene from* Stagecoach *(Wanger/UA 1939).*

Stagecoach makes a brief nod towards the law and order issue with its sub-plot involving the Ringo Kid, but, substantially in content, and certainly in its sweep and feeling, it belongs to the first category. It makes a good staging-post for discussion of this most romantic of Western forms, which seizes on the visually strange and exciting notion of emigrants (some of them urban and literally pale-faced) trekking into a harsh, hostile and virtually Stone Age environment. It's a category which proves to be largely the province of the late John Ford.

Stagecoach makes much capital out of an early means of communication. Ford used it as a symbol —there is nothing more striking, as an image of loneliness, than a long-shot of a coach twisting its way through the arid and fretted South-Western landscape—but also as a box for shaking and mixing human drama. The combination is devastating. Despite some carping criticism that there is just a little too much contrivance about the selection of passengers riding in the 'box', that they look as if they've been handpicked for contrast and for drama, *Stagecoach* always repays another look. It still works admirably. Time takes little away from it.

Stagecoaches had played their part in the Western story from the mid-century years. The famous Wells Fargo firm began operations in California in 1852 and John Butterfield, who started life as a stage driver, was to see his company, the Butterfield Overland Mail Co., get a subsidy from the government for providing a service that would fulfil the needs of the Californian miners.

They wanted closer, quicker touch with the east, and the government, not without certain fears that the Californians, headstrong and independent, might go their own way entirely, if they did not get satisfaction, soon co-operated. By the autumn of 1858 Butterfields had organized stations all the way along the 2,812 mile route from Tipton, Missouri to San Francisco.

Each station provided horses and mules, often half-trained, it was said, for the relay service, and rough and ready meals, often half-cooked, for the hardy passengers.

Hardiness was essential if you wanted to survive a stagecoach journey. It wasn't just a matter of Apaches—'Seen any Indians?' was a stock greeting at the way-stations—or latterday highwaymen trying to ease the coach of a possible gold consignment.

From accounts that have been left of these hair-raising rides along routes no better really than ruts, where speed was all (it had been stipulated that the whole journey must be done in 25 days) physical endurance, it would seem, was even more important than the nerve to fight off marauders.

ABOVE *Disaster comes to the Cheyenne tribe in* Soldier Blue *(Avco-Embassy 1970).*
BELOW *This time the Indians are triumphant at the famed Battle of the Little Big Horn. The defeated loser, General George Custer, takes it out on his guide, Dustin Hoffman, in* Little Big Man *(Stockbridge/Hiller 1970).*
OVERLEAF *Poster art in the movies,* The Good Guys and Bad Guys *(left);* John Wayne and Rod Taylor in The Train Robbers *as advertised in France (right).*

JOHN WAYNE · ANN-MARGRET
ROD TAYLOR

LES VOLEURS
DE TRAINS

Butterfields were to be challenged by the Pike's Peak Express Co. who wanted to operate what was known as the Central Route, and to advertise this in 1860 they started the Pony Express—fast teenage riders carrying the mails between St. Joseph and San Francisco in 10 days. It was too costly to be a success and was stone dead after 18 hectic months. Butterfield later sold out to Benjamin F. Holladay, perhaps the most striking of all stagecoach entrepreneurs who became fabulously successful before also selling out, to Wells Fargo in 1866.

But already telegraph wires were clicking out messages and the sound of the steam train was just around the corner.

Ford's resounding salute to the bone-shaking era has, as we have said, some carefully selected 'characters' boxed in for a troublesome ride. They are not characters, save perhaps for the drunken doctor, in the usual Ford sense of beloved eccentrics. They are highly contrasted 'types' who, by some alchemy that the movie develops, *do* grow to some extent into credible human beings.

Apart from the drunken Doc (superbly played by Thomas Mitchell), there's the mysterious southern gambler (John Carradine), a pregnant wife (Louise Platt) joining her soldier husband, a whisky salesman (Donald Meek) who could kid anyone at first sight—especially an audience—that he's a parson, a whore with a heart of gold (Claire Trevor), and an absconding banker (Barton Churchill).

Andy Devine is in the driving seat, George Bancroft, as a U.S. Marshal, rides shot-gun and keeps a wary though fatherly eye on the Ringo Kid (John Wayne) who has come along for at least part of the ride.

Two things are at once apparent. Ford is employing a dramatic device for which there is plenty of precedent—compressing diverse characters into a confined and highly charged situation in the certainty of reactions, and, secondly, that the Claire Trevor character is the spitting image, as they say, of Maupassant's tart, Boule de Suife.

Geronimo will be the catalyst for this load of combustibles. He's on the loose again and the escorting cavalry have already had to say their farewells to the coach party.

The story would seem to be a natural for any Western producer. Ford had bought the original story—*Stage to Lordsburg*, by Ernest Haycox—and

with Dudley Nichols had amplified it. He had his troubles, however, in launching the picture.

Ford was insisting that Wayne should have the part of the Ringo Kid. But the fact was that for some 10 years Wayne had been doing nothing but quickie Westerns and producers were a little chary of using him.

Walter Wagner, however, took the risk which, as it turned out, was hardly a risk at all, with such a fine balancing cast and the care and attention that Ford lovingly languished upon the production. Wayne learned that he had got the part one day while they were relaxing on Ford's yacht.

Stagecoach leaves a whole host of abiding impressions. There is the dramatic black and white photography taking advantage of every trick of light and shade in the wonderful Monument Valley location. It was the first time that Ford had used this setting within the Navajo Indian reservation around and about the Arizona–Utah state dividing line. The eroded lunar landscape has its own beauty and its own menace and these two qualities are reflected in the film. Cloudscapes and silhouettes—these linger on.

There's the feeling of panic engendered when the news gets out that Geronimo is once more back in the raiding business; a feverishly communicated feeling of 'Surely it's getting late in the Western day—but here we are, no longer safe again.' There's the climactic chase of the coach which has passed into cinematic language, with Yakima Canutt, the best man in his line of business, organising the stunts and the horsey virtuosity; the interplay of characters as perhaps best illustrated at the Apache Wells way-station where the drunken doc is sobered up and his morale boosted sufficiently to deliver a baby. And then that most memorable sequence with a twilight quality all its own where 'Duke' Wayne walks his girl back 'home' to a street of shame.

Holes have been shot into *Stagecoach* although it has never really been riddled. Bill Hart, the stickler, once said that in real life there would have been no prolonged chase culminating in that thrilling bugle-announced rescue by the cavalry. Geronimo and co., would simply have shot the horses and that would have been that.

Ford's typically laconic riposte was to the effect of 'Yeh, but that would have meant the end of the picture.' This isn't as cynical as it sounds. It was another way of saying that art isn't life, it's selected

A painful scene from Cahill *(Batjac 1973), another John Wayne movie.*

*Robert Shaw (*left*) as the flamboyant cavalry general and (*below*) Custer & Co. mixing it with the Indians. Both scenes from* Custer of the West *(Security Pictures 1966).*

life, and that he was telling a story, or interpreting a legend, however you cared to look upon it.

He could have posed the old question: what *is* truth? One answer to this is that it is more likely to be found, not in broad statements, but in significant detail. Certainly this film abounds in bits of evocative detail, which give a feeling of time and place and of being there. Particularly the offbeat 'contrast' touches. For instance, the daunting confrontation of the tight-lipped ladies of the Law and Order League—a hint here of the frontier already yearning for respectability—and Claire Trevor's 'woman of shame', while the soundtrack adds its ironic comment with a hymn of the period, 'Shall we gather at the river?'

It's curious that the musical score of *Stagecoach* has not received half the attention it deserved. It's an artful mixture of all American ballads, blues, love songs, with the occasional hymn thrown in.

The cavalry made a sensational entry in *Stage-coach*. Ford was to paint them in more fully in his later films. Their role in the Western story was profoundly important. Like most military roles of its particular nature it was demanding and thankless.

Their brief, which was a large enough brief for anyone, was to police the West and it had been allotted to them because no other branch of the U.S. Army, be it infantry or artillery, could be expected to cope with a foe who were rated the best light cavalry in the world and where the theatres of war were enormous, mainly barren places.

'You could never fight nor pursue them with infantry and artillery,' said one U.S. Congressman at the time. 'Out of reach of the guns of the fort and these corps might as well be a thousand miles distant. They can never come up with the enemy.'

Safeguarding immigrants on the move, settlers, miners, in hostile territories where frontiers were ever changing, and with forces never numerically adequate—this was the task. Additionally, they had the irksome duty to keep whites out of Indian land.

Life for the men in blue was hard and, by any sorts of standards, unrewarding, save for the pure adventurers. The climate was harsh so that it was struggle enough to survive in good health, let alone fight. Discipline was also harsh. Flogging could be administered (up to 50 lashes) for desertion, and lesser punishments for lesser crimes included being suspended by the wrists or thumbs.

And the force was mainly composed of immigrants, with Irishmen largely to the fore (Ford of Irish origins always makes play of this). Gary Cooper, in one of his few comments on the Western scene, once lamented that not enough cinematic attention had been paid to the part played by immigrants—'gutty old characters who helped build the West'.

The whole strategy was based on a string of simply constructed forts, which were rarely as well fortified as an armchair warrior, or cinema fan, might imagine. Life for the cavalryman, of course, included those much screened patrols, but he spent far more of it on plain garrison duty doing drills, guard duties and general labouring. For recreation there were paperback novels (they might at a later date even have included the dime Westerns and thereby furnished a ribald means of comparison), old newspapers and the occasional fort dance.

Little of this, save for some honourable exceptions, comes through in the proliferation of frontier stories that the Western has to tell. One might have expected a closer, more intimate look at the cavalryman in those several films that have covered that final, fateful and shaming meeting of General George Custer and the Sioux and Cheyenne under Sitting Bull, Crazy Horse, Gall and Two Moon at Little Big Horn in the summer of 1876.

These films included *They Died With Their Boots On* (1941) which starred Erroll Flynn and Olivia de Havilland, and which wasn't even very accurate about Custer, let alone individual members of his command, and *Custer of the West* (1968), starring Robert Shaw (this was filmed, incidentally, in Spain) which was not particularly illuminating.

ABOVE *and* BELOW *Two scenes from* My Darling Clementine *(20th Century Fox 1946), John Ford's splendid version of the legendary Battle of the O.K. Corral.*
RIGHT *Victor McLaglen (left) and Dick Foran as a pair of 'old sweats' in John Ford's* Fort Apache *(Argosy Pictures/RKO 1948).*

The cavalrymen get a more honourable deal from three films made in succession by John Ford —*Fort Apache* (1948), *She Wore a Yellow Ribbon* (1949) and *Rio Grande* (1950).

These are quite properly referred to as his 'cavalry trilogy' as they deserve to be considered as a body of work dedicated to a particular theme, that of the life of the cavalry and their role as frontier protectors in times of Indian uprising.

Fort Apache is about the tensions in an isolated fort—social and military-hierarchy tensions, and, ultimately, the purely military tensions that arise when the commanding officer is transparently ill-fitted for his command.

Henry Fonda, an embittered colonel who can't get over losing his Civil War rank as general, arrives at the desert outpost to take over from the experienced Indian fighter, John Wayne.

He is arrogant, brooking no advice, and further alienates the frontier veterans by refusing to countenance the romance of his daughter (Shirley Temple) with a young officer (John Agar) who happens to be the son of the regimental sergeant major (Ward Bond). Shirley and John, incidentally, were real life man and wife at the time *Fort Apache* was filmed.

There are nice touches in the film here about army traditions. The N.C.O.s are well represented by Victor McLaglen (Ford's favourite Irish cavalry sergeant), Dick Foran (a former 'singing cowboy') and Jack Pennick.

The inevitable climax concerns, of course, the new C.O.'s arrogance and ignorance leading him into military disaster—a head-on clash, despite all warning, with Cochise who is commuting 'twixt Arizona and Mexico. There are echoes here of the General Custer debacle at Little Big Horn.

Fort Apache is a neat and well balanced piece of work, based on James Warner Bellah's story *Massacre*, and it makes a worthy contribution to Ford's cavalry films, but the lynch-pin of the trilogy is undoubtedly *She Wore a Yellow Ribbon* which remains for many their favourite Western movie.

It has charmed its way into this position. It would be hard to uphold any claim to supreme excellence. Ford has surely done better himself, unquestionably with *My Darling Clementine* (1946) and *The Searchers* (1956), yet one has to admit the undoubted merits of *She Wore a Yellow Ribbon*. Even the usual criticism launched against it— that it is over-sentimental—can be dismissed at the start. Certainly Ford *can* be sentimental but only when the springs of good honest sentiment run dry and lose their inspiration. This never really happens in *She Wore a Yellow Ribbon*. Deep-dyed romantic in concept and execution it lilts along as if in time with its theme tune and is often quite incredibly beautiful. Never have the cavalry been braver images. Landscapes, men and horses are all decked out with fetching flourishes.

But garrison life still comes alive in the naïve rivalry of two young lieutenants (John Agar and Harry Carey Jun.) for the favours of the major's daughter (Joanne Dru), and some knockabout interaction between two hardcore professional soldiers—the captain (John Wayne) and the sergeant (Victor McLaglen).

The captain is about to retire but he has one last soldierly chore before becoming a civvie. This is where it all becomes sympathetic rather than sentimental. One identifies with the veteran—after all, retirement is no less sad through being honourable—and hopes and prays that he will prove himself one more time before hanging up his gold-braided blue.

And this is what happens. The chore—escorting the major's wife and daughter from the danger area—misfires when they find the stage station burnt out by Indians; they have to return to the fort, flanked by menacing warriors, and to think again.

Climactic action seems a long time coming in this film which is due to its concern with the retirement theme, but naturally, when it does come it involves the captain's last successful stratagem before his farewell.

Ford's cavalry trilogy is, in its way, just as much McLaglen's trilogy, for he appeared once again in *Rio Grande*, still superbly filling the bull-necked sergeant part, still providing the Ford horse-play comedy element with just a touch of parody, still, one might add, probably fulfilling Ford's own particular vision of an Irish N.C.O. of the times.

The McLaglen sergeant seems drawn on the broadest of lines, but in retrospect, one realizes that somehow, paradoxically, he has infused a remarkable degree of realism into the three pictures. They would not be the same without him.

LEFT *This scene from Ford's* She Wore a Yellow Ribbon *(Argosy Pictures/ RKO 1949) seems to confirm an old soldier's maxim that the longest mile is the last mile home.*
ABOVE RIGHT *John Wayne added to his growing stature by his performances in Ford's* She Wore a Yellow Ribbon *(Argosy Pictures/ RKO 1949) and* Rio Grande *(Argosy Pictures/Republic 1950) (below).*

Rio Grande has a very strong domestic flavour. John Wayne is a cavalry officer with family problems that have well and truly come home to roost. He's a northerner who, not surprisingly, has fallen out with his wife (Maureen O'Hara), a southerner, because of his full-hearted efforts in the cause of the Union during the Civil War. These include the hardly forgiveable burning down of buildings on her family plantation.

He has trouble enough in his professional life. He is in the familiar outpost situation of having to cope with Apaches with one hand tied behind his back. The warring band make their raids and then disappear over the border into Mexico. Treaties between the two governments bar any chases over territorial boundaries.

Into this vexing situation come the added complications of the arrival of his son (Claude Jarman Jun.) as a rookie on the post, and, later, the advent of his wife, determined to effect her son's discharge.

Everything, domestically and militarily is, of course, resolved successfully and, indeed, predictably (Wayne does get a chance to smoke out the Apaches in their own territory and becomes reconciled with his wife when he is posted abroad as a military attaché), but it is the texture of the film that gives it its relish—the interplay of Wayne and Jarman, the quirky supporting contributions of such as Ben Johnson, Harry Carey Jun., Chill

Wills and McLaglen, members of what affectionately came to be known as Ford's Rolling Stock Company (actors suiting his style and requirements, whom he favoured again and again).

The John Wayne denigrators who sneered 'he's only playing himself' when the veteran won an Oscar for his performance as a fat old Westerner in *True Grit*, a film of the late sixties, might advantageously consider a look at *She Wore a Yellow Ribbon* in which Wayne plays a character 'getting on in years' and invests the performance, dating back almost two decades, with real authority and dignity.

The three films, even considered singly, but certainly judged in toto, give a feeling of frontier military life, however coloured by a director's highly personal viewpoint, that has hardly been approached, let alone surpassed. An entirely different flavour permeates an outstanding Western that is also historically orientated. This is Howard Hawks' *Red River* (1948), a film which is spectacle at its best although spectacle is by no means all of it. Spectacle needs a sharp eye and a clear mind about the overall purpose to make its point and if these are missing the result can sometimes be quite abysmal. One thinks of *The Alamo* (1960), John Wayne's directorial tribute to the struggle for Texan independence, in which noise and confusion battered the ears and clouded the understanding.

The flavour of Hawks' film is that of dust, and,

LEFT *A typical shot of John Wayne in Howard Hawk's dusty, gritty cattle-droving epic* Red River *(Monterey/UA 1948).*
RIGHT *John Wayne in his own* The Alamo *(Batjac 1960).*

What gave Red River *(Monterey/UA 1948) its remarkable feeling was the tense, love-hate relationship of John Wayne and Montgomery Clift.*

when it gleams, it gleams with sweat. It is epic in its sweep and the size of its canvas but the canvas is packed with hardbitten detail rather than romantic flourishes. Based on a *Saturday Evening Post* story, *The Chisholm Trail*, this is a tough, astringent tribute to one of the determining phases in the economic growth of the West.

Cattle were almost an embarrassment in immediate post-Civil War Texas. Most Texan cowboys had become soldiers and so the cattle, neglected and left to roam of their own free will, had multiplied accordingly to an estimated 5 million longhorns.

Yet in the north, where immigrants had also multiplied, there was a dearth of beef. A reception area of stockyards had been established in Chicago, railways began pushing westwards across the Great Plains and their railheads were open invitation to the dollar-hungry, cattle-embarrassed Texans.

But, in between, lay mile upon rugged mile of harsh, often hostile country seemingly unable to support the passage of great herds.

It wasn't, however, impossible. In late 1865 a half-breed by the name of Jesse Chisholm had taken a wagon from Kansas to Fort Worth, Texas, marking his route all the way by mounds of earth. Jesse also brought back news that cattle were fetching up to as much as fifty dollars a head in the north.

It was enough to put a glow into all depressed Texans. It was more than sufficient to give the Cherokee half-breed a place in history. The trail he blazed, the trail that cattle were to follow, would always bear his name. A quarter of a million cattle were to ford the Red River in 1866 bound for the northern stockyards.

The 'cowboys' drove them and the life they led was exhausting, often monotonous, but perhaps almost as often packed with as much peril as any adventurer would want to accommodate. Lack of sleep, stampedes, the perpetual rounding up of

strays, persuading great herds to cross intimidating water, persuading Indians, forcibly sometimes, from depleting the herds. At the end of it all the primitive 'cowtown', payday and the melting of pay in dance halls, brothels and saloons dispensing bad whisky.

This was the drover's lot and many a film has in one way or another sought to testify to it. *Red River* is the definitive rendering.

It spans about twenty years in all, beginning 14 years before the Civil War. John Wayne and that unmatched 'old timer' Walter Brennan are part of a wagon-train bound for California, but en route Wayne and his 'pardner' take a notion to head south, instead, for Texas.

A decision surely blessed with premonition, for that night they see fires that can only mean that the train has been attacked by Indians. Any smugness they feel is, however, soon dissipated when they themselves are attacked and the cattle driven off.

Red River is a Western just as much concerned with human relationships and their tensions as with spectacle and action—a hallmark of Hawks' films— and this element is introduced when the pair meet up with a boy leading a cow. The boy confirms the wagon-train massacre, and the boy and the cow from then on are included in the partnership. This is not only a key-point of the narrative but also a highly symbolic moment.

In Texas the Wayne character flourishes. He lords it over a cattle empire but by the time the boy, now grown into manhood, in the person of Montgomery Clift, has returned from the wars (Civil), who wants beef in Texas? (Incidentally, Clift, a well established Broadway actor, was a comparatively recent recruit to movies at that time. *Red River*, in fact, was only Montgomery's second film. He was hailed as a Star of Tomorrow as a result of his fine performance.)

And so we are back with our genuine old-timer, Jesse Chisholm, and his beckoning trail to fortune. Wayne and Clift decide to take it.

'Duke' Wayne—King of the Westerns.

A stampede, an eye-taking river crossing, the rescue of a beleaguered wagon-train—these are the main set-piece spectacles, but the whole film is powdered with dust and resonant with the sound of hooves and peculiarly effective in its almost documentary detail of the day by day working routine of the drovers.

Everything was big-scale in this production. Hawks used the San Pedro river in south Arizona as 'stand-in' for the real life Red River. But it was dry more often than not and so five dams had to be built to get enough water for the famous cattle-crossing sequence.

Nine thousand head of cattle were assembled and shooting their crossing took three days and 30,000 feet of film shot from 15 different camera sites, one of them secured in the river itself. All for eight minutes on the screen but certainly eight of the most impressive minutes in terms of spectacle in the history of cinema.

Similarly with the equally celebrated stampede scenes. Thirty-five highly experienced cow wranglers provided the expertise behind this big, bold splurge of spectacle which took 10 days to film. Hollywood stuntmen doubled for the drovers we see in peril at the feet of the maddened herd. Some were injured but none seriously.

Visually impressive though this film is, however, *Red River* makes its fiercest demands in its human tugs and tensions. It is soon evident that the cattle boss is tough to the point of obsession. It could be argued that only men of this mettle could have handled and survived the first pioneering cattle drives. One of the drovers (John Ireland) wants to make for Abilene but gets no change out of Wayne. When the cattle stampede Wayne goes to 'gun-whip' one of the hands but Clift intervenes. Wayne, it is now evident to all concerned, is going to drive his men just as hard as he intends to drive the cattle.

There are desertions and there is the inevitable 'mutiny' headed by Clift who, strictly against the deposed boss's wishes, decides for Abilene. The similarity apparent now between *Red River* and *Mutiny on the Bounty* (1935/1962), between the whip-flailing cattle boss and the flogging-obsessed Captain Bligh seems almost too pat for mere coincidence. Some theme-borrowing seems indicated. It's by no means unheard of in Westerns— the prime example was Japan's *Seven Samurai* (1954) which became Hollywood's *The Magnificent Seven* (1960).

When Wayne seeks to meet up with Clift in Abilene and there kill him it looks as if a soupçon of Greek tragedy is added to the mixture for the boy is surely an 'adopted' son. But there's a soft core to the hard ending and one is left wondering for the moment why Hawks was so insistent on his ambivalent, love-hate relationship for a film that might have rested its case on a fine scenic handling of an epic theme.

The answer, as once suggested by Charles Schnee, co-writer of the screenplay, was that Hawks was totally antipathetic to any idea of a run of the mill hero and villain—'he wanted men of flesh and blood'.

The villain as such doesn't exist in *Red River*. There are black sides to the Wayne character, but also heroic aspects, man struggling against the elements, as Schnee puts it.

It follows from this concept that the sustained tension in the film does arise directly from the ambivalence of the relationship and of the man himself. A stereotyped villain quickly dealt with is soon forgotten. But although Wayne and Clift may break up their climactic fist fight with mutual grins—the apparent soft core—one is left with the feeling that although the tension between them may be subdued it will never be finally resolved. And, because of this, as well as its dust and hooves and details of a cowboy's day—the whole great raw sweep that Hawks has stamped upon it—*Red River* will remain a film with a unique flavour. It has, and will continue to have, its own special niche among honoured Westerns.

If the stagecoach is an essential piece of ritual in Western lore the wagon-train looms even larger. It creeps its way through many films, ponderous and somewhat pathetic in its seeming vulnerability, the women in their poke bonnets riding, the men walking alongside the oxen teams, and the children skipping along picking prairie flowers. Safety, so the image says, can only lie with the true professionals, the weatherbeaten wagon-master and perhaps a couple of scouts reassuring in buckskin. And not all that reassuring when the camera cuts to Comanche riders making a menacing fresco of a jagged skyline.

Independence, Missouri, was the launching point for wagon-trekking which got its initial impetus in the early 1840s. They called it Oregon Fever and thousands were infected in the Mississippi Valley by tales of fertile lands in the far west. They sold up their farms, packed their belongings in prairie schooners and began the laborious 2,000 miles from Independence to their Promised Land along the Oregon Trail, leading through prairies, deserts, mountains, canyons and hostile Indian

ABOVE *A typical John Ford comedy touch in* The Wagonmaster *(Argosy Pictures/RKO 1950).*
BELOW *Richard Widmark, a firm Westerns' favourite.*
RIGHT *Robert Mitchum, who has also made his mark in Western films.*

country. It was a trip that would take over three unforgettable months.

The Covered Wagon might well be thought to have said the last word on this epic pioneering theme since it was devoted to it. But what it said was disappointing, and, in fact, it could be held that no film on this subject has given total satisfaction.

How The West Was Won (1964), which surely aimed at being the definitive Western, failed totally on this count, let alone the segment it dutifully granted to the wagon-train story. Having three directors couldn't have helped. The veteran Henry Hathaway, responsible for some good Westerns, was in charge of the wagons.

The Way West (1967), which was directed by Andrew V. McLaglen, was a good honest effort. This had Kirk Douglas, Robert Mitchum and Richard Widmark making the trip as dynamic master-mind, tough pioneering farmer and blasé half-breed scout, respectively. Its weakness was probably an emphasis on the characterizations and clashes and the starry 'mix'.

Probably *The Last Wagon* (1956), Delmer Daves' somewhat neglected account of a 'baddie' (Richard

Widmark) seeing the wagon-train through, is better than most.

John Ford paid the wagons his tribute of a special picture, *Wagonmaster* made in 1950 and this has received much acclaim and his own accolade of being one of three movies which most of all matched up to his original conception.

The trek here is in 1879 and the wagons are full of Mormons, their chattels and their aspirations for their Promised Land.

They are led by Ward Bond (another fine member of the John Ford Rolling Stock Company) in the role of an Elder, and the 'professional' side of the project is in the hands of two free-wheeling youngsters (Ben Johnson and Harry Carey Jun.).

The voices of the Sons of the Pioneers come constantly piping through the sound-track with hymns and folksy tunes, and whom do we meet en route? None other than that hammy old actor we last saw spouting Shakespeare in the same director's *My Darling Clementine*.

The wagon-train also gathers to itself an excrescence of outlaws, rather in the unwonted way that a ship gathers barnacles, and ultimate action depends, of course, on their removal.

It's a lovely-to-look-at film, full of a marvellous buoyant optimism, and it is easy to understand why Ford found it so satisfying. It never breaks faith with the mood and style set in the first few sequences. But one is left wondering whether the ultra-romantic best suits the chosen theme.

The wagon-train experience must have been one of the most physically demanding and nerve-wracking ordeals that man (with his womankind) ever set himself. It must have been riddled with doubts—was I wrong to sell up everything and come? how can we hope to survive? how will we cope the other end?—almost every other aching step of the way.

Yet none of this feeling really comes through in *Wagonmaster*. The journey—such is the general ebullience—doesn't strike one as particularly hazardous. It could be, of course, that the Mormons were so 'high' on religious spirit that this tended to act as an anaesthetic. In other words their reactions weren't those of normal human frailty. If so, Ford was right and the doubters were wrong.

What is beyond doubt is the right and proper ebullience, especially at first meeting, of Ben Johnson and Harry Carey Jun. (son of the silent Western star). This is the essence of light-hearted adventurous youth, particularly one feels of Western youth of those extraordinary times. It's a remarkable relationship and it remains lodged in the mind.

One John Ford film that it would be difficult to overpraise explores and exploits one pioneering aspect that normally only gets implied or passing attention. This is the sense of isolation, loneliness and constant threat of peril that was the lot of the settler and was inherent in his environment.

The Searchers brings the feeling to focus in the story of the abduction by Indians of two white girls and the long hunt for them that becomes a personal crusade. 'Masterpiece' isn't a word to be used lightly but few would quarrel about applying it here.

Personal accounts, in the form of letters, and family folklore, are vivid reminders of what it was like, especially for a woman, in a humble farm cabin, when rumour was rife of an Indian uprising. Her man would be out on the farm, maybe away for days because of the distances involved, and with no near neighbours to share her fears she would have the terrible task of trying to keep them from her children. While she was out milking she would watch for smoke on the hills and, if it snaked up, wonder whether it was some normal blaze or an Indian signal, or some homestead burning. It was the loneliness that bred such fears although some of them were only too well founded. The Western pioneering woman knew that, if Indians struck, death, in fact, might not be her immediate fate. There were too many well-known cases of abduction, followed possibly by torture and death, or more likely by ill-treatment and humiliation as a sort of slave camp-follower of the tribe.

In the Cheyenne raids on settlements in 1864 one woman, subsequently released, told how after being forcibly 'taken as wife' by an old Cheyenne chief, she was later traded to a Sioux and then twice again. The Cheyennes, she added, had tried to buy her and her child back so that they could burn her. Two other women captured during the same raids gave evidence of similar treatment. Another captive had taken her own life.

The Searchers is about just such a raid and the terrible obsession of a man who seeks not only to rescue captives but to exact fearful vengeance.

John Wayne (the name Ethan suits him well) comes riding back from Confederate service in the Civil War, three years after it's over, to the Texan ranch he co-owns with his brother (Walter Coy). There's bitterness and mystery about the man. There are gold double eagles in his saddle-bags and there's a clammed up look in his eyes that says whatever he's done, or whatever he's been through, he's telling nothing. It's obvious, though, that he's glad to be home, that he's quite fond of his brother's wife (Dorothy Jordan), but he hates the fact that they've adopted a Cherokee half-breed (Jeffrey Hunter) into the family.

When Ward Bond, a preacher-cum-Rangers' captain, drops in to form a posse, Wayne goes along with him, only to find later that they've been decoyed away by Comanches. He gets back to learn that his brother, his wife, and their son have been killed and their two daughters have been abducted.

Wayne sets out to find them, accompanied by Hunter and Harry Carey Jun., as the son of a Swedish farmer. It's a long, long search which takes them five years before one of the girls who has grown into Natalie Wood is retrieved by Wayne—as a squaw perhaps somewhat reluctant to be rescued. Again there is historical antecedent. The white Cynthia Ann Parker, captured at the age of nine by Comanches, bore their greatest leader, Quanah Parker. When she was 'recaptured' she missed the old free life of the Plains and pined away and died.

It's a great rambling film, befitting a rambling journey, but, because of clever cutting back to the ranch house base of the enterprise, it never loses narrative tug. Even more important, in retrospect, is the mood engendered by Ford, using to the full his two greatest gifts in Westerns—his sense of time and place and his rare knack of conveying the look of it.

Nothing he did as a landscape artist matches at depth the brooding quality of this film. Ford ranged far and wide for his fine effects. He used once again his favourite Monument Valley with its buttes and mesas and rosy spires, went on location also to Edmonton, in Canada, for the buffalo-hunting scenes, and got his telling snowy landscape shots in Gunnison, Colorado. It is a huge poem that cries 'wilderness' and the images sustain it. Whether it's parched, arid trekking, or plodding through northern snows, the eye is constantly told about space, loneliness and isolation.

The lesson is there right at the start—the territory so big, the settlers so pitifully few. And so conscious of their isolation. This is underlined in the early scene where the family know by instinct that the sort of trouble they've dreamed of a thousand times, the kind of death they've died in imagination, is finally skulking just around the corner.

To this is added the quirky style, behaviour, and look of rural, isolated people best summed up in the presence of Ward Bond's top-hatted old-timer. The folksy comedy touches—Vera Miles, the Swedish rancher's daughter, making her play for Jeffrey Hunter, captive in a bathtub; Hunter's hilariously violent reaction to the situation when he returns from searching to find that the daughter, fed up with waiting, is on the brink of giving herself, if not her true heart, to 'another'. All this has 'frontier' written all over it in the very best John Ford calligraphy.

But the essence of it all is sadness with a distinctive lemony flavour and it is distilled most truly in the character of Ethan, played by Wayne with such monumental insight. Ford called *The Searchers* the tragedy of a true loner and this is what Wayne, a very much underrated actor, conveys—a man chewing on some private, bitter cud, of which his detestation of Indians, carried to the point when he wants to kill his captive niece when he realizes that she has been 'Indian defiled', is just a convenient means of expectoration.

Ford's treatment of the Indians in this film is less superficial than in some previous offerings. The Comanches' own grievances are touched upon and there is real pathos in the Indian attempts to preserve their children from the wrath of the avengers.

A more sympathetic objective look is not entirely a latter day attempt to make amends. In the early days of the silents two highly accomplished directors—D. W. Griffith (Daddy of them all) and Thomas H. Ince, who both made valuable contributions to the Western, had put the Indian point of view.

ABOVE *The camera again alights on the horrific in* Soldier Blue *(Avco-Embassy 1970)*.
BELOW *Dustin Hoffman wields the scalping knife in* Little Big Man *(Stockbridge/Hiller 1970)*.
OVERLEAF *The moment of truth for an Indian maiden in* Soldier Blue *(Avco-Embassy 1970)*.

LEFT *Henry Fonda, an actor who has given style and distinction to the Western film.*
ABOVE *James Stewart and Jeff Chandler eloquently pleaded the Indian cause in* Broken Arrow *(20th Century Fox 1950).*

Ince's *The Indian Massacre* (1912) sought to present the Indian destiny in terms of stark tragedy while Griffith's film *The Massacre* (1912) with story implications of the Little Big Horn battle was also 'fair' to the Indians.

This, of course, was swimming very much against the tide of cinematic treatment over the years. The only good 'un's a dead 'un was the more downright expression. If not so explicit, other films cast the red man as a kind of generic 'enemy', an indeterminate mass of war-bonnets, that could loom as inchoate and inconvenient as a thunder-cloud. It was a tradition that was based in the loose generalities of the commercial conveyor belt entertainment which was also, of course, main base for the Western.

And yet the well documented Indian story was one of obvious genocide—the destruction of a culture and traditional means of life (the buffalo is an example), the theft of land and the breaking of treaties, the debauching of health and values (alien diseases and bad whisky).

Contrary to popular conception this was not without challenge at the time. . . .

'Is it a light thing to drive a people from their native land? There was never an exile of any other race to whom the American heart did not warm. There was never even a foreign nation struggling for the peaceful possession of its fatherland with which we did not sympathize. . . . We profess to place highest in the category of human virtues the love of native land. How comes it, then, that Americans can favour forcing our "wards" to leave the "rocks and rills", the "woods and templed hills" that they love?'

This was an American writer putting it both fairly and squarely as far back as the latter part of the 19th century.

Delmer Daves' *Broken Arrow* (1950), based on Elliott Arnold's *Blood Brother*, has a quiet word to say for the Indians.

This sees James Stewart as Tom Jeffords, an intrepid frontiersman, trying to patch up peace with the Apaches under Cochise with Jeff Chandler,

ABOVE Run of the Arrow *(RKO/ Globe Enterprises Inc. 1957), starring Rod Steiger, was also sympathetic to the Indians.*
BELOW *Richard Harris in* A Man Called Horse *(Sanford Howard 1970), a film that delved surprisingly deeply into Indian customs.*
RIGHT *Schoolma'am, Carroll Baker, an Indian sympathizer in John Ford's* Cheyenne Autumn *(Ford-Smith 1964).*

a wooden sort of actor, in this role giving probably the most sympathetic performance of his career. Stewart and Chandler soon strike up a man-to-man understanding and the Indian chief allows the mail riders to go through Apache territory unharmed although he preserves the right to continue war against the U.S. soldiers.

The strength of this often lyrically photographed picture which will always have an honourable place among Westerns lies particularly in the touching dignity of Stewart's love and marriage to an Indian girl (Debra Paget). Indian haters, of course, stir up the usual sort of trouble and Stewart's bride becomes a victim with all the consequent poignancy for which the film is best remembered.

The protest in the film is somewhat low-key and the Indians tend to be literary in conception rather than actual. But the heart of it for once is in the right place. The playing is sincere and controlled throughout. If Chandler rings oddly true in feathers, so does the frontier-garbed Stewart, an actor with much wider range than he is often given credit for. Few movie actors can distil genuine pathos out of quietude so expressively.

Run of the Arrow (1957), a film directed by Samuel Fuller, has Rod Steiger taking an Indian wife (Sarita Montiel) and here the Indians are less idealized. Steiger, deserter from the Southern cause, is a highly credible character, tough and able to effect a compromise with the Sioux until he finds one aspect of the culture he can't stomach, let alone assimilate—that of skinning a captive alive. He still, however, rides out of the picture with his Indian wife alongside. Whether she will assimilate what *she* finds in a different culture remains unanswered.

Even this more realistic film doesn't really get to the heart of Indian culture. Perhaps *A Man Called Horse* (1970) which starred Richard Harris, as a Sioux-captured British lordling, gets nearer to it.

John Ford dealt with one of the perennial Indian tragedies in his *Cheyenne Autumn* (1964), the wasting away of a tribe in an uncongenial pen called a reservation and its efforts to take matters into its own hands. Indians, to use a modern term, had become redundant; that was their true tragedy. They were unwanted in what the whites wanted to make of the West and so they were 'placed' and disposed of, thereby suffering the usual 'redundant' maladies of physical and moral debilitation.

The Cheyennes, 1,500 miles away in Oklahoma from their Yellowstone home, had seen their numbers depleted from one thousand to less than

three hundred in the course of a disease-ridden year. With these sorts of statistics it was as much a matter of simple logic as an act of desperation when they upped and left one night, bound on foot for their old hunting grounds, probably knowing full well that the cavalry would chivvy them, as they did, all the way.

An epic in real life. Would the master epic-maker match it? In purely visual terms the answer was 'yes'. But somehow Ford never wholly got to the heart of the matter although the intent was there and at times this is a most impressive and moving film. Richard Widmark is the officer who is as sympathetic as uniform allows and Carroll Baker, the Quaker schoolteacher whose sympathy abounds. But an improbable captain of cavalry (Karl Malden) doesn't help and neither do some off-beat antics in Dodge City between James Stewart as Wyatt Earp and Arthur Kennedy as Doc Holliday, splendid though they may be in their own right.

Films had long sheered away from one aspect of the American treatment of Indians—well-authenticated episodes of brutality which equalled anything that the redskin had perpetrated in the way of massacre. Quite rightly it was held to be a touchy subject in pure commercial terms. There were few dividends to be got, at least until recently, from fouling one's own nest in public.

And yet it was all there to read about. . . .

The world knew of the bloody incident on December 28, 1890, at Wounded Knee Creek, when trigger-happy soldiers with Hotchkiss quick-firers had slaughtered about 200 Sioux—women and children as well as men among the victims.

Less well-known, however, were the happenings at Sand Creek, Eastern Colorado, on November 29, 1864 when an estimated 500 Cheyenne and Apache Indians, about half of whom were reckoned to be women and children, were killed in their village by militiamen, although said to be holding a white and an American flag. The American force, cavalry and artillery numbering some 750 men, were led by Col. John M. Chivington, a 'muscular Christian' of the not uncommon 19th century kind who found no moral conflict in simultaneously toting Bible and musket.

The local Coloradoan soldiers had without doubt been severely provoked. The Cheyennes and their allies had been raiding settlements and stage stations carrying away women and children. But the Indians had been making their own protest about being forcibly shifted from their tribal territories and at the time had sued for peace and had returned to the Sand Creek reservation.

The massacre was terrible. One soldier who testified before an investigating committee told how women and children had been scalped and their bodies mutilated in an obscene fashion.

Arthur Penn's *Little Big Man* (1970) hardly ranks as a traditional Western. It takes off on the wings of fantasy, purporting to present the life and Western times of a frontiersman (Dustin Hoffman) who has lived no fewer than 121 years. As such the story rambles over various episodes in Western history and makes no uncertain mark when it deals in an unsentimental way with such a massacre of Indians by whites. It is most movingly done.

Two faces of Dustin Hoffman in Little Big Man *(Stockbridge/Hiller 1970); as the 121-year-old survivor of Custer's last stand (left), and as the town drunk (below).*

But there is no question that the biggest impact in this context was made on the general public by Ralph Nelson's *Soldier Blue* (1972) which was much criticized for gratuitous violence, suspect motivation and inept handling. There's a degree of truth in these objections—it is impossible, for instance, not to believe that outright shock figured largely in the makers' minds . . . the severed heads and the spouts of blood.

It was sights like these, however, that so affected the hardened soldiers at Sand Creek that they felt they must speak out against them. *Soldier Blue* makes no bones about dealing directly and comprehensively with this untold aspect of the Western story. As such it has its place in any anthology of 'historical' Westerns.

The makers have said that it represents a re-creation of both the Wounded Knee and the Sand Creek happenings but there's more of Sand Creek in the look of it and certainly the commander of the American force, played by John Anderson, is based on Chivington.

The story, leading up to the climactic massacre, has the hero (Peter Strauss) learning against the grain all about soldiering as he helps to escort gold across Cheyenne territory. With the Cavalry unit is Candice Bergen, a former white captive of the Cheyennes and wife of their chief. The Bergen role introduces another shock element. She is earthy

to the point that even Calamity Jane might disown her. The Bergen performance is so overblown that it is difficult to assess this 'earthiness' rationally. And yet one wonders—where lies the truth about frontierswomen? Did they all seek to reconstitute the East in parlours, which is the implication in so many cinematic townships? It's doubtful, knowing the life they led. Hardship tends to coarsen and hardship was their lot.

The Bergen character harbours no ill feelings against Indians who had treated her well while she was among them. And these feelings somehow survive a Cheyenne attack which leaves Soldier Blue and herself as the only survivors and which, for ferocity, is only matched by what is meted out in the final set-piece. As far as ultimate sympathy for the Indians goes, this attack is an alienating error.

The plot then casts Miss Bergen as spokesman— at least at heart, for she is deploringly inarticulate— for the Indians, and as an eventual and unavailing means of warning them of their likely fate.

It's a theme that deserved abler handling. If this had been possible the world would have been spared that telling and shaming comment from a tennis star of South American origins. He loved, he said, watching Western films on television. But he always turned them off while the Indians were still winning.

LEFT *Moment of strange reunion between Dustin Hoffman and Faye Dunaway in* Little Big Man *(Stockbridge/Hiller 1970).*
RIGHT *and* BELOW *Two scenes from* Soldier Blue *(Avco-Embassy 1970), starring Candice Bergen and Peter Strauss.*

The Fastest Guns in the West

DESPITE some scepticism which has tended to the other extreme—Gary Cooper himself said that he doubted whether more than three per cent of cattle-range war fatalities had actually occurred—the fact is that the classic 'growing-up' period of the West was lawless by any standards.

Lawless, that is, Indians apart. Lawless in the sense of a family squabbling as only families know how. The great preponderance of Western films, a few good, but most shoddy or indifferent, have been devoted to this theme of domestic strife. The miracle of it all is, therefore, that shots and films

LEFT *Gun-blazing Randolph Scott in* Frontier Marshal *(20th Century Fox 1939)*.

BELOW *Prelude to a shoot-out in Henry Hathaway's* Rawhide *(20th Century Fox 1951)*.

Two scenes from The Ox-Bow Incident *(20th Century Fox 1942),
forerunner of the 'psychological' Western, starring Dana Andrews, Henry
Fonda and Anthony Quinn.*

stand out (and some do brilliantly), when the whole scene tends to become a blur of swinging saloon doors, bottle-skidding challenges in long bars, vanishing tricks on the part of cowed citizenry, sidewalk duels, and impromptu rodeos by drunken cowboys whooping it up in pathetic little townships.

Exaggeration may have piled up on exaggeration over the years but the basis of fact is genuine enough. In the prevailing circumstances the wild and woolly West could hardly have been otherwise.

The people themselves were largely restless individualists, with a gleam of distant Eldorado in their eyes. Plain greedy—many of them. It was once unkindly said that if a sizeable proportion of the 'pioneers' had had true grit, to borrow the title of a latterday Western, they would have rested their wagons halfway and got on with their pioneering. But always the crock of gold in the Western sky lay over the hill.

The advent of the cowboy was hardly designed to usher in a decade of peace and general goodwill. In the early days, in his role as drover, the Texan cowboy, still Johnny-Reb in sympathies, was not likely to take kindly to northern authority, es-

pecially in those Kansas towns which were the aiming point for those lonesome, laborious drives —Abilene (the first), Ellsworth, Hays City, Wichita, Dodge City. . . .

He was a man with a gun, and that didn't help. Fisticuffs, which might have kept down the death rate, didn't become him, had never been part of his make-up. He relied on the invention of Samuel Colt, the six-shooter which had quite a long history and had experienced a number of modifications before it played its part 'in bringing peace to the West'—perhaps the most grimly ironic of all claims.

So there he was, a man with a gun, and money in his pockets, looking for fun in signally funless places, and in his free-and-easy, open air way, a despiser of bourgeois values as represented by shop and saloon keepers. As they grew up, the townships really did, at heart, want to take on the bourgeois values of the east—lace curtains, a piano in every parlour. The women saw to that.

And when the cattle scene changed or, rather, drifted from droving into ranching and the cowboy blended into other landscapes, such as Wyoming and Montana, he remained the same character he had ever been.

This is far from saying that within every cowboy there was a villain trying to shoot his way out—there were enough assorted villains of other kinds only too eager to do their bit—but the cowboy, nevertheless, could play other roles.

He could become outlaw—and did; there was no one better technically equipped to become a cattle rustler. And he was there, anyway, in such substantial numbers—it has been estimated that some 40,000 went north—that on the law of averages he was a basis of lawlessness when that was the prevailing climate. It was the fag-end of wartime (the Civil War) when, as after all wars, values were loosened, particularly any value put on human life, since recent experience had officially said otherwise.

It was a time and place for gambling since gambling always waxes strong when there is money to burn and little else to do for recreation. Every lonely war experience bears this out. But gambling, with the tensions involved, is seldom on the side of peace.

So the people were there and the times were ripe. And issues weren't lacking, quite apart from those that were purely personal. There was a mining frontier and a cattle frontier. One led to outlawry

pure and simple and the other a warfare that was never simple—battles over who owned whose stock; battles by cattlemen against sheepmen, and homesteader farmers (the cowboy-belittled 'sod-busters') and the ultimate unpleasantness about barbed wire.

And seldom, if ever, was there enough law to go around. This resulted in town marshals who were sometimes shady characters themselves, doubling as lawmen and gamblers and not without vested interest in the whores. Then there were the unofficial lawmen—specially hired gun-fighters brought in by really frightened communities. And if there was no law-representative handy whatsoever, the final act of desperation occurred when citizens took the law into their own hands.

Lynching, the summary action of so-called vigilante committees, was always cropping up in the never ending squabbles about who owned whose cattle.

It's a long time since it was made but it is doubtful whether there has ever been a better movie to illustrate this than William Wellman's *The Oxbow Incident* (1943), called *Strange Incident* when first shown in Britain.

Based on a fine, thoughtful novel by Walter Van Tilburg Clark, the theme here is one of tragic misunderstanding, the sort of witches brew of error, impatience and intolerance, which must have often characterized Western rough justice.

Mob fury besets a little cattle-town like a fever. Most citizens seem only too eager to join a man-hunt for the murderer of a rancher. Henry Fonda and Henry Morgan have to go along with the tide, if only for the fact that, as wanderers passing through, they are not above suspicion themselves.

The unofficial posse, berated all the time by a blown-up bullfrog of a major (Frank Conroy)—his true military worth is always suspect, as also is his taunting of his gentle son—finds three suspects asleep. Dana Andrews seems to be in charge and no one could be blamed for suspecting one of the men, a Mexican played by Anthony Quinn.

The trio all die on a tree despite Andrews' pleas for a 'fair trial'.

Then, riding back, the lynch-mob gets the news that the rancher is still alive and the real villains have been taken. All that remains to be done—and there is an ironic savouring to this—is for Fonda to read Andrews' dignified, moving last letter to his wife.

The Oxbow Incident was never 'box office'. As things were at that time it's hard to see how it could ever have nurtured this hope. But it lives on still when a multitude of money-makers have sunk with hardly a trace. Seen today, it's dated only by the odd look of its 'exteriors' which have studio written all over them, and which give it at times a certain staginess.

It makes its point, however, as well as it ever did. It's not only about the social injustice of instant justice; it's also about human nature, all its oddities, frailties and the perils therein. It's often said that it laid the beginning of the psychological Western. That's perhaps too grand and ambiguous a claim. What it does possess to a marked degree is acute observation, and a subtlety that is never obscure.

Fonda, that most subtle of actors, is largely responsible. You see the whole thing, as it were, through his eyes, but he leaves you guessing for quite a while as to where *exactly* he stands. (Glenn Ford is another actor in Westerns who profitably plays secrets.)

Dana Andrews did nothing subsequently to match the sensitivity he showed as the unfortunate 'necktie party' victim in *The Oxbow Incident*.

The Colt revolver was a tool and the more you study the men who used it at a high professional level the more it becomes obvious that they were also tools, sometimes unwittingly, sometimes (ac-

cording to Western films) quite the opposite. Necessary tools, necessary men in a very compressed package of American history. They have their brief moment on the stage and then it's time to take their leave, preferably with their boots on, knowing, or not knowing that they've done the job that history actually required, but that history, in fact, won't thank them for it.

Fonda, again, puts this over perfectly in Edward Dmytryk's *Warlock* (1959), a neatly turned, well-scripted, unpretentious Western, entirely in the classic mould. Here Fonda is a hired gunfighter brought in specially, and most temporarily, one always feels, to quieten down a town plagued by cowboys, some of them with outlaw affiliations.

Spruce and spry as ever, Fonda is caught by his girl-friend to be, busily practising with his gun, discreetly outside of the town he must tame.

'I'm a simple man, handy with Colts,' he says to the girl, and then goes on to explain: 'just like you practise on the piano, ma'am—I practise on the Colt.'

He's full of professional-folksy-gunman philosophy . . . (on killing) 'It's clear the first time—it's never clear afterwards. It's only the rules that matter. Hang on to them as if you were holding an egg.'

Every word he says, every calculated ploy, shows that he's marvellously clear-eyed about his situation—that today he's wanted, that tomorrow he won't be—because he's an old pro and it's all happened before.

But, of course, there's another side of it—*is* there any place, any retreat, any home of retirement, that an inevitably tiring gunman can move on *to*?

This predicament is best conveyed, explored and given its full tragic weight in Henry King's *The Gunfighter* (1950).

In some ways it is the predicament of every 'champ', every 'star', although not in the same brutal terms. There's always the talented or over-confident youngster who just can't wait in the wings any longer as contender for the title. He wants to take over the mantle long worn by the master. He has to prove he's best and, in the case of the gunman, this can only be done with a gun.

And so Gregory Peck, wearing his reputation as the fastest gun in the south-west territories like a heavy load, enters each bar warily when he needs a quiet drink, knowing full well the reaction—fear, respect, perhaps admiration, and certainly the intervention in some form or other of a young upstart with itchy gun-fingers.

The pattern is set early on when Peck has to shoot a boy (Richard Jaeckel) in self-defence. And so a feud begins—you feel it's only one of many—

with the three brothers of the boy (Alan Hale Jun., David Clarke and John Pickard) hell-bent for revenge.

Peck deals with this situation, at least for the moment, sighs and then moves on to a place that passes for home. Here is his wife (Helen Westcott) and his son, who won't, however, be providing him with a welcome since in the eight years that husband and family have been apart the wife has been trying to build a life of their own.

Here also is a sheriff (Millard Mitchell) formerly engaged in Peck's outlaw activities, but now reformed, and an old girl friend (Jean Parker) ready to help him in anything that concerns him most. His actual concern is reconciliation with his wife and a new life together. There is a tentative rapprochement but, of course, there is another of those young contender interventions, this time in the person of Skip Homeier, and a sly shot from the young 'un puts paid to the old 'un's late dreams of reclamation.

He does, however, have the last word. He dies with the satisfaction that no revenge could be sweeter than the fate that will now be the lot of the killer, and he says as much. From now on the youngster will be on trial. Hunted by others with youthful itchy fingers he will have to defend his new-won reputation.

In its way, *The Gunfighter* can also claim the last word on its subject. Comparatively unheralded and unsung at the time, it grows in stature as the years go by. Honest and understated, its virtues positively gleam when compared, say, with a strident over-stated Western such as Nicholas Ray's

Johnny Guitar (1954) a film in which Joan Crawford, always larger than life, throws in enough of the high-powered stuff to evoke shades of a Victorian melodrama. It's odd to note that a bit of a cult has formed around this somewhat embarrassing picture. It should surely be evident that however cleverly a camera is used it is not equipped to cope with corn.

A sombre, tragic but above all gritty and down-to-earth film, *The Gunfighter* bluntly lays it on the line—this was how it mostly was, being a champ with a gun; sad, nasty and inevitable.

Peck strikes the right note from his first edgy entry. He is superb in his brief and nervy reunion with his small son, impressed like the rest of the local kids by the fact that Jimmy Ringo, the gunfighter, is in town.

The same elements, even the same impressionable boy, are present in another great Western, that perhaps wears the 'classic' accolade better than any other. This is George Stevens' *Shane* which, unlike *The Gunfighter*, was never treated as anything else but 'great'. 'There never was a picture like *Shane*,' ran the publicity fanfares.

Well, that was a challenge to all critics. But most of them left the previews looking thoughtful.

Many cinemagoers have argued, and the argument is bound to persist, that *Shane* is the greatest Western of all time. But it's bound to be an arid argument. Taste, perhaps particularly in Westerns, is highly personal. All that one can really hope for is a top-of-the-heap consensus. A sound case *could*, however, be made out for another contention— that *Shane* is quite the most all-round *satisfying* Western ever made. It combines so many elements that are 'classically' required and combines them so well. Of all Westerns it would be certain of a pride-of-place showing in our celestial film festival.

The photography is both beautiful and effective, whether it's carefully composed landscapes and group sequences (the funeral of Elisha Cook Jun. for instance), or action, shot against harsh settings (Mr. Cook's demise at the hands of Jack Palance, or the Alan Ladd/Van Heflin pastoral tree-grubbing scene).

It's a romantic film, certainly, and yet it is full of integrity about time and place and probably comes closer than any other movie to giving the feel of

LEFT *The sad and sorry end of a gunhand as depicted by Gregory Peck (comforted by Millard Mitchell and Jean Parker) in* The Gunfighter *(20th Century Fox 1950).*
BELOW *Wary-eyed Gregory Peck drifts into his last town.*

ABOVE *Alan Ladd and Van Heflin have the same end in view in George Steven's* Shane *(Paramount 1953), but there's a little difference about the means.*
RIGHT *Ernest Borgnine in a typical violent scene from* The Wild Bunch *(WB/Seven Arts 1969).*
OVERLEAF *A well-composed scene from Andrew V. McLaglen's* Firecreek *(WB/Seven Arts 1967), starring Henry Fonda and James Stewart.*

that hoary old Western issue, the clash between cattlemen and sod-busters.

It contains that mystical element that runs like a thread through the Western story—the stranger who rides into town at exactly the right moment that history requires him, fulfils his destiny and then rides on. And it's a film, too, that's profound and explicit about gun-fighting. The gunmen loom over it large . . .

Shane (Alan Ladd) just happens to have ridden into a bit of Wyoming frontier—the film was shot at Jackson's Hole, Wyoming—at a time when a group of homesteaders led, if that is the right word for the loose association, by Van Heflin, are being bullied by long established cattlemen, under Emile Meyer.

The mysterious stranger seems glad of a job with the homesteader and you can see that the farmer's son (Brandon De Wilde) is impressed by his

buckskin gear and his gun and that the farmer's wife (Jean Arthur) is not unaffected. But this is no ordinary hired hand. He carries world-weariness heavily on his shoulders. He is wary and sad. He has quick nervous reactions to particular noises—such as the unseen, innocent snapping of a gun-breech. He is a gunfighter . . . or has been in the past.

When the other side specially import their own man—Jack Palance, a sinister figure all in sable—it's all teed up for an ultimate showdown. On the way there's that impact-making gunning of Elisha Cook Jun., and some stirring knockabout stuff between Ladd and one of the cattleman's cow-hands—the excellent Ben Johnson, much favoured by John Ford.

If the choice and general get-up of Palance was a stroke of genius in this film it should also be added that George Stevens either picked on Ladd

LEFT *Robert Mitchum in* The Good Guys and The Bad Guys *(Ronden 1969).*
ABOVE *The famous funeral scene in* Shane *(Paramount 1953).*

at some personally bitter-sweet point of this actor's career or coaxed out of him a performance quite above his normal level. He genuinely does look haunted, burdened with unease—all, in fact, that the part requires. It's the best thing by far that Ladd ever did.

It is the acting, throughout, so solid and perceptive, that perches *Shane* on its pedestal. The reaction of a child to adult violence—Brandon De Wilde gives the whole glint of it. The natural resentment and exasperation of a cattleman with foot-slogging homesteaders—Emile Meyer manages this enormously well. Your sympathies, since this really is a law and order issue, should be on the other side, but you have a sneaking feeling for him —and for his kind.

After all, they were taking the brunt of it when their bit of country was ringing with war-whoops. Meyer still nurses the hurt caused by a Cheyenne arrow.

But, above all, it's the drudgery and patience and fortitude of the sod-buster's life, implied so impressively by Van Heflin and Jean Arthur, that illumines this fine picture.

A traveller who went through the small-farming areas during the times they first met the plough, wrote that he could imagine nothing more desolate and vacant than the sight of the land first broken— just black land as far as one could see, with nothing growing at all.

The humble sod-buster had to have ineffable pluck, and, primarily, faith in those days. It was an act of profound faith to visualize the ugly black land one day verdant with wheat.

When Miss Arthur looks at Ladd, glamorous if world-weary in buckskin, and then looks at her husband, so patently a good and worthy man but stuck on his awful bit of land, you can almost hear her plead: 'Take me out of here. Let's go roaming!'

The irony, of course, is that all the tired gunfighter really wants is to roam no more.

So gunfighter Ladd played his role in a Wyoming valley and the implication is that he left a better place behind him.

John Ford in *The Man Who Shot Liberty Valance* (1962) took similar facts for his text, but sprinkled them with doubt and sadness.

Nostalgic, sour and powerful, it is one of the most memorable of all his Westerns—and a far cry from those dashing sabre-waving, banner-dancing pieces of early ebullience. It's triggered off, and that's the right phrase, as it turns out, by flashback. The old device works well in the hands of the master. In fact, Ford couldn't have got the feeling he's after in any other way.

It's a mixed feeling—compounded of pride, regret, and a sense of the inherent injustice of life, and certain forebodings about the future.

When Senator James Stewart, looking every inch the revered veteran political figure, gets off a train at a small Western town with his good lady (Vera Miles) you can tell by the way his eye roves for and rests on bits of time remembered that this is very much a sentimental journey. He's come to pay his last respects to a friend of the long, long ago—a small rancher in those days, played by John Wayne.

Dissolve into the distant story—presenting young tenderfoot lawyer Stewart, eagerly intent on bringing Eastern law-books to bear on the problems of the West. His first taste of the West is a sound beating up by a man called Liberty Valance (Lee Marvin at his sadistic whip-flailing worst) who is a gunman employed by powerful cattlemen, and who, incidentally, has the unhealthiest contempt for law, whether it be Eastern or what passes for it in the West.

Nor does Stewart find any real custom even among the law-abiding. He starts his career, in fact, as a kitchen hand in a café where he's been taken by John Wayne, following his nasty experience with Marvin. Ford is at his 'domestic' best in this café which is run by a Swedish pair (John Qualen and Jeannette Nolan) and where Stewart's wife-to-be is one of the employees. Stewart, wearing an apron contrasted with Wayne, pure frontiersman, is something to see in that kitchen. And there's always an edge to their meetings.

It isn't hard to guess that before long the waitress, Wayne's girl, is going to fall for the legal eagle who takes on her education.

Stewart eventually hangs up his sign in the office of the local newspaper editor, Dutton

Two scenes from John Ford's The Man Who Shot Liberty Valance *(Ford/Paramount 1961).*
LEFT *'Duke' Wayne turned in one of his finest performances.*
BELOW *The trio who battled in their different ways for the future of a frontier town; James Stewart, Lee Marvin, John Wayne.*

*Two scenes from Fred Zinnemann's
classic* High Noon *(Stanley Kramer
1952), starring Gary Cooper and Grace Kelly.*

Peabody, a typical Ford 'character', played by Edmond O'Brien, and from then on it's the story of a territory growing up and seeking statehood, with Stewart maturing, too, as the natural leader of 'civilized' law and order aspirations.

But none of it could have happened without the removal of Marvin. Stewart confronts him and the bullets fly but the bullet that actually drops him comes from Wayne's Winchester in the shadows. Stewart goes to Washington on the strength of ridding the territory of Liberty Valance, but *he* knows that the shot was fired by Wayne. To his credit, he hates the reputation.

It's another film about the right man being in the right place at the right time in order to advance the course of Western civilization. But in this case the right man never gets his just deserts—if he ever wanted them, because the Wayne character in his way is just as much a part of the Old West as Marvin.

Herein lies the bitter essence of the film. Wayne, at heart, is as contemptuous of what Stewart stands for—talk and conferences and thick legal tomes (all urban perquisites)—as the gunman is.

And through him you feel Ford saying that the hard men who had it the hardest on the frontier are soon forgotten, and some of the frontier's simple virtues have been buried with them. For what? you almost hear him asking, probably taking a jaundiced look at neon signs, desert-devouring

freeways and other tokens of 20th century progress. The mind goes back and back to *The Man Who Shot Liberty Valance*. Skilful, undoubtedly, but it is also honest, unpretentious and deeply moving. In no other Ford Western does the audience feel so involved. The playing is brilliant—from the smallest role to the beautifully interpreted ambivalent relationship of Wayne and Stewart.

If the role of the official lawman—the town marshal—was ambiguous (apart from his varied interests the chances were that during his career he'd seen both sides of the law)—it could also at times be a lonely one. Citizens might yearn for law and order but they were realists and were always sizing up the balance of power.

If the lawless seemed particularly powerful the lawman could look in vain for civic support of a practical kind when the chips were down. This is a theme exploited by two outstanding Western films.

Fred Zinneman's *High Noon* (a 1952 film) is possibly the most celebrated Western along the whole crowded route. It's the one film that comes quickest to mind when you ask non-Western cinemagoers to name a picture from the genre. Highly-stylized—almost, perhaps, to the point of contrivance—carefully and beautifully shot, it possibly owes its abiding popularity to a combination of three things—it's a suspense film in the real sense (Hitchcock wouldn't have disowned some of the mechanics on the way); the dearly beloved set-piece climax of the gun duel never got better or more thoughtful treatment; it has a theme tune that persistently whines its way into the subconscious.

Most people first remember the Dimitri Tiomkin theme tune, then Gary Cooper stalking down the lonely street. The bits and pieces gather from there.

The tune, fittingly enough sung by an old Singing Cowboy (Tex Ritter) got its 'plugging' from an afterthought. The idea, in the first instance, was to use it normally—that is merely with the credit titles—but cutter Elmo Williams, who edited magnificently, thought it could help all way through and how right he was, as far as the general public were concerned. There will always be a body of opinion, however, that will insist that the 'don't forsake me' wedding day lament handicaps rather than helps this fascinating law and order movie.

Incidentally, *High Noon* was aided—and this is probably the right word in this respect—by another afterthought. Producer Stanley Kramer, at a late stage, thought it needed a little more suspense, and so inserted those shots of a clock that are always nudging the audience about Cooper's imminent ordeal.

The film gave him his greatest Western role. He actually took a salary cut. This wasn't as generous as it sounds, for he also took 'a piece of the picture' which was something quite new in those times and must have been one of the most profitable starry gambles of all time. By such means the resourceful Mr. Kramer was able to lead in his winner for the modest cost of around 750,000 dollars.

High Noon cashed in on the theme of the old pro literally sticking to his guns, when, honestly, he has no real need to do so—it's Cooper's day of retirement and also his wedding day. Why doesn't he just stow his bride into his buckboard and get out of town?

It also ties in that other factor that recurs in Westerns—rather like a bad and shaming dream—the 'cowed citizenry', the little men showing their enormous capacity for survival by turning their backs on trouble, integrity, and an elected representative.

Cooper, on a blazing June morning in 1875, has just married Grace Kelly. The bride feels doubly blessed. She's got her Gary (it's Will Kane, actually) and this is the day he will hang up his guns. She has firm Quaker convictions and never did fancy herself as a lawman's wife.

But, while it's all being celebrated a badly shaken stationmaster (Ted Stanhope) bursts in with quite the wrong kind of wedding telegram. It states that an outlaw (Ian MacDonald) whom Cooper had put behind bars six years ago for terrorizing the town has been pardoned. The stationmaster adds that three members of the terror gang have already arrived in town—their object a reunion with the pardoned man who will get off the train at noon, and presumably a final settlement with the marshal.

The early merit of the film which immediately gives it credibility is that minds are shown to be in the melting pot, that decisions have yet to crystallize. The marshal, like a sensible man, *does*, in fact, put his wife in the buggy, but then like a man of honour but *also* a sensible man (for the gang will surely hunt them down wherever they go) changes his mind and heads the horses back to town.

A bride, especially a Quaker bride, can't quite see it this way on her wedding day so she hands him her own ultimatum—if he won't go away with her she'll go alone by train—the one that leaves at twelve.

Everything on this torrid, dusty morning there-

fore hinges on midday—hence Mr. Kramer's insistence on his clocks. From this point onwards *High Noon*, although it remains completely classic in Western terms, faithful to period and concerned with an indicative historical situation, takes on wide and profound implications. It's about group cowardice and short-term interest—particularly the treachery of so-called 'good' people. 'Law abiding,' you feel, doesn't mean what it should mean. When a pack of people decide that they must passively refuse to support the law for reasons of personal preservation, who, in fact, are the outlaws?

Thus the marshal's predicament. He is an embarrassment to everyone, from Judge (Otto Kruger)—*he's* leaving town—to the humblest citizen of Hadleyville.

Only one is ready to give assistance and he melts away when he finds there'll be no other volunteers. The marshal's immature deputy (Lloyd Bridges) is willing to take over his job—again, provided Cooper leaves town. But this is plain ambition at work.

In the end, it's the wife who, against her strongly held convictions, comes to his aid. She has character in a town with an all-round lack of it. No wonder when they finally climb on the buckboard they give no one or nothing a last backward glance.

Will Kane in *High Noon* is a very worried man. John T. Chance, the sheriff, played by John Wayne in Howard Hawks' *Rio Bravo* (1959), is faced with a similar situation but always makes you feel that somehow he'll cope. Not in any 'B' feature sense of a sheriff's omnipotence but because of sheer experience and expertise.

Wayne, holding a prisoner (Claude Akins) on a murder charge in a Texas border town, waits for the state marshal to take charge of him. But the the prisoner's brother (John Russell), a local ranching V.I.P., wants him free and is determined to release him by any method possible.

The obvious method is the traditional one— hired gunmen—and, in effect, the sheriff becomes a prisoner himself, in his own town. Townsfolks' backs are again turned the other way. But in this instance the lawman is not absolutely without help—although at first glance the help available is unprepossessing. The two deputies are a crippled veteran (Walter Brennan adding another to his superb gallery of 'ornery old-timers) and a pretty hopeless drunk with a past 'fast' reputation (Dean Martin). And when a mild-spoken, seemingly much too tender tenderfoot (Ricky Nelson) offers his aid this again doesn't impress.

But the whole point about this cleverly con-ceived movie is that this unlikely trio *do* in fact have something to offer when the cards are dealt. Like the sheriff, they're professional people, and what Hawks seems to be saying is that whatever the odds, such people will always have the edge. Wayne expresses this with every look and movement. Like a great professional ball-player, he takes things step by step, playing it the only way he knows how, whatever the state of the game.

And in the famous sequence when blood dripping into beer warns Dean Martin of peril above from a wounded gunman, the partially written-off drunk dredges up flair from his better days and saves the situation by reflex action.

Rio Bravo is a beautifully controlled film, with its action thoughtfully placed and never too fast to savour. And it's one of those Westerns that does gain from a feminine role. Angie Dickinson playing Feathers, the gambling gal, enriches the mixture with a nicely judged performance.

One of the more surprising things about the cast selection for *Rio Bravo*—which, incidentally, says much for the Howard Hawks way with actors—was the choice of Martin and Nelson for two such important roles, particularly when one considers the whole range of experienced 'Western talent' available.

Martin hadn't long made the change from music and comedy while Ricky Nelson at that time was just a well-known 'pop' star, about to try on the shoes of Elvis Presley who was due to keep a call-up date with Uncle Sam. But the relative inexperience in the Western form doesn't show at all. The performances in *Rio Bravo* are all admirably balanced. The combination of 'Duke' Wayne and Hawks seems to have rubbed off on all concerned. 'Duke', in fact, was more than mere example. He went out of his way to impart Western know-how to the tenderfoots, how to handle a horse and a gun and so on. And he made a commemorative gift to Ricky Nelson of the ancient and revered stetson he'd worn in *Stagecoach* and *Red River*.

Law and order Westerns have never had to rely on the fiction-smith pure and simple. The classic period had enough characters colourful enough in their own right. And if, at first sight, they might have appeared just a tinge or two anaemic, the newspapers of the time and fiction writers were always willing to help out with the legend. The truth was that actual performance seldom matched the reputation. This is not to be wondered at since reputation, either by print or word of mouth, became so highly coloured.

But there *was* a man who wore the title of Wild Bill Hickok and his life *was* eventful by any standards.

He was born James Butler Hickok in 1838 and his life seems to have been a pattern of 'scrapes' involving the death of people, with his own role most times ambiguous. In the summer of 1861, for instance, while working as a wagonmaster, he and some friends killed three men at a stage station. It seems to have been one of those 'personal' matters which were always flaring up at the time and were clouded over by gun-smoke. The smoke apparently never did clear away over that particular battle for he was found not guilty.

The Civil War saw Hickok scouting and spying for the North, but hardly was it over when there was another 'personal' unpleasantness. This time he gunned down a fellow-gambler, Dave Tutt, at Springfield, Missouri. But once again he was cleared. Two years on saw him as sheriff of one of the cattle towns, Hays City. Here three men fell to his guns. Next port of call was notorious Abilene itself where as City Marshal he killed a gambling thug called Phil Coe and, incidentally, wounded, by accident, one of his assistants.

By all accounts, he had presence—'star quality', one might say today. He was tall, smartly dressed, and wore his brown hair at a 1973 shoulder length. His moustache flowed and there was a general, pantherish grace about the man that must have

John Wayne and Walter Brennan in Howard Hawk's Rio Bravo *(Armada 1959).*

been, in those rowdy saloons, as intimidating as his pistols. And, temperamentally, Bill was 'real cool'. Small wonder that the East demanded to see him in person (they already, of course, knew much of him through print).

Wild Bill did, in fact, go East, and became an 'actor', following, one supposes, the showbiz trail already blazed by Buffalo Bill Cody. But the year 1876 saw him back in the West—this time in the gold mining centre of Deadwood in the Black Hills of Dakota. And here, while he was engaged in his staple livelihood (gambling) he was shot in the back of the head on August 2nd by a cowardly character called Jack McCall.

This was a man certainly worthy of the very best screen attention. But the strange thing is, that, apart from a few honourable exceptions, the colourful characters of the vintage Western era, have rarely brought distinction to the Western film. How many would one include in one's favoured list of really outstanding Western movies? And this is an observation not concerned with such films' obvious scant respect for the facts—sometimes carried to the point when characters are shuffled between situations and incidents like pieces of pasteboard in a gambler's pack— meeting people they'd never met in places where they'd never been.

Wild Bill, who was consciously theatrical in real life, has no grievance (wherever he is) about the amount of attention paid to him but he could very well carp about the quality. From Bill Hart onwards several of the early stars gave portrayals but probably the most definitive remains the Cooper version in DeMille's *The Plainsman*, a stagey and imperfect film at that. Strange, too, how Wild Bill has changed in character over the years. For *Jack McCall, Desperado* (1953) Hickok, who had always been hero, or semi-hero, was quite a bit of a villain.

Billy the Kid, too, has cause for complaint. As well, perhaps, he's not here to seek redress, for in real life his way of seeking it was brutal and brief. This most notorious and publicized of teenaged killers, born William Henry Bonney (or Henry McCarty)—most probably in Brooklyn—in 1859, was on the run from a murder charge in Arizona when he got a job on the ranch of a recently arrived Englishman, John Henry Tunstall.

Tunstall and a lawyer named Alexander McSween, who were most likely acting for a cattle king, John Chisum, were developing business in Lincoln County, New Mexico, as a challenge to a powerful near-monopolist group controlled by James Dolan and John Riley.

Tunstall was murdered and this started the famous Lincoln County war in which Billy played his part. Range war, therefore, made him, or destroyed him, as you happened to see it. He was small and mean and teenage pimply but seems to have had undoubted affection for Tunstall whose murder he sought to avenge. By the end of this 'war' he was reckoned to have killed 21 men but it's an unlikely figure. By the end of the war, also, he'd embarked on a new career, as a rustler. He was captured in 1880, sentenced to death, but he shot his two jailers, Bob Olinger and James Bell, and escaped.

A gallery of 'Billy the Kids'.
ABOVE *Paul Newman in* The Left-Handed Gun *(WB/Harroll 1958)*.
BELOW *Jack Beutel (threatened by Jane Russell) in* The Outlaw *(RKO-Howard Hughes 1950)*.
RIGHT *Johnny Mack Brown in two scenes from King Vidor's* Billy The Kid *(MGM 1930)*.

He was free only for three months. Sheriff Pat Garrett, a former gambling and drinking friend, caught up with him and killed him.

The Garrett-Billy relationship is almost always the keystone of Billy the Kid movies.

King Vidor's early sound version, *Billy The Kid* (1930), had Johnny Mack Brown, who was later to become a 'B' Western favourite, as Billy and that all-round heavy, Wallace Beery, as Garrett. Hart was a consultant on this picture which has a certain integrity that still earns respect. Beery, oddly enough, who could 'ham' a part up to destroy all belief in it, played Garrett on a quiet note, and most effectively.

Certainly this was a better movie than the 1940 offering with the same title, directed by David Miller, and Robert Taylor and Brian Donlevy in the main parts. Robert Taylor as a nasty adolescent psychopath? With casting like that it never had a hope.

Neither was there much credibility about *The Outlaw* (1943), directed by Howard Hughes, which seemed largely concerned with the projection of the more prominent charms of Jane Russell.

The Left-Handed Gun (1958) suffered perhaps from a feeling of surfeit—surfeit of Method acting and also of the preoccupation of books and films with 'mixed-up kids'.

This was a pity for if ever there was a candidate for the category of 'mixed-up kid' it must surely have been William Bonney. From all accounts of his behaviour, style and actions, Bill was the original. With his background and experience he could hardly have been anything else; everything points to an extremely disturbed personality.

Paul Newman played him this way in Arthur Penn's fascinating film which had its faults—extreme historical purists will be glad to mention them—but which in the opinion of many was unfairly received at the time.

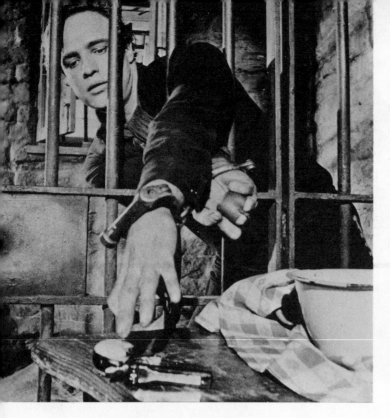

ABOVE *Marlon Brando reaches for freedom in* One Eyed Jacks *(Pennebaker 1958)*.
RIGHT *Tyrone Power with an ominous background in* Jesse James *(20th Century Fox 1939)*.

It seemed to many that *One Eyed Jacks* (1961) drew upon the Garrett–Billy relationship for its inspiration. This film, which had undoubted visual attributes, had Marlon Brando both as star and director. Brando took over as director from Stanley Kubrick at an early stage and the costs soared mainly because, it has been said, of Brando's passion for 'improvizations'. It had a mixed critical reception.

There is one film, however, that raises the much used story to quite a different level. This is Sam Peckinpah's *Pat Garrett and Billy the Kid* (1973) a rich, haunting, yet demanding work that, above everything else, sees Billy as a creature of his day and age.

He is by no means made a wholly sympathetic character, but who *was* sympathetic in the New Mexico of 1881? Peckinpah has most of his characters dyed with violence and sniffing the prevailing air of corruption—the chief protagonists, their squalid henchmen, even the onlookers.

Where and what is the law? No one seems to know or care. Garrett and Billy have seen both sides, like almost everyone else.

And amid the confusion and violence that is the legacy of range war there is no gleam of purifying light in the efforts we see being made to clean up the territory. The powers that be want Billy out of New Mexico, not for ethical reasons, but rather so that things can be neatly tidied up for the oncoming business exploitation.

Garrett is the man made sheriff to hunt him down and thereby the man who compromises . . . 'This country's getting older and I aim to grow old with it . . . there's an age in a man's life when he has to consider what's going to happen next.'

But Billy can't compromise. It's not his way. 'Billy, they don't like you to be so free!' proclaims the Bob Dylan theme song, summing up why the power men find Billy so irksome. Perhaps that's why Garrett who has sold out to power is in some ways a reluctant hunter. He salutes Billy's spirit— his very own personal declaration of independence —but he knows it's not the spirit of the new times.

It says much for Peckinpah's way with actors that he gets such admirable performances out of the comparatively inexperienced Kris Kristofferson, as Billy, and Bob Dylan, as Billy's mate. It says just as much for his Westerns acumen that he relies even more heavily on experience. The well-tried James Coburn is both solid and subtle as Garrett. And then there are the others who know their way around Westerns so well—Katy Jurado, Slim Pickens, R. G. Armstrong, Jason Robards, Jack Elam, Chill Wills. There's not a single performance here that isn't a rounded-off portrait in its own right.

It all adds up to a richness in characterization that is matched by the richness of marvellously composed scenes in which interiors and exteriors alike have been put together with loving care and attention to detail, whether it's a big set-piece 'shoot-up' or a close-up of a can of preserves— how such a can looked in 1881.

Garrett's hunt for Billy is told mainly in set-pieces and it has to be said that Peckinpah makes little narrative concession to an audience in the way they are strung together. Anyone unversed in the idiom or the Lincoln County war chronicles could be pardoned for finding *Pat Garrett and Billy the Kid* hard going. But for the out and out Western fan this is a most memorable movie.

Billy the Kid was hardly an example of the strictly commercial outlaw, the type who robbed stages, banks, trains etc., and made much less from this risky business than is often believed. Characteristic and more successful than most were the James boys, Frank and Jesse, who hailed from Missouri. Their service as guerillas on the Confederate side in the Civil War most probably gave

them a taste for the lawless life. And, in fact, in company with other guerillas they led the same kind of life when the war was over—their raiding now focussed on banks.

The James boys became associated with four notorious brothers, the Youngers—Cole, Jim, John and Bob. In 1876 three of the surviving Youngers were taken following a raid on a bank at Northfield in Minnesota. Jesse James was heard of again about three years later and Frank seems to have rejoined him a year after that.

A train robbery in 1881 resulted in a reward tag of ten thousand dollars being placed on the head of each of the brothers. The following year saw the end of Jesse—shot by Bob Ford, a member of the gang. Frank, who survived two trials—he was acquitted on each occasion—lived on until 1915.

Jesse James has become a name to conjure with. Perhaps it's the ring of it. Perhaps the name itself is enough and is best left to flit through the imagination. For realization, at least on film, never quite matches the imagining. Fred Thomson starred in a version of the story in 1928, but best remembered is another oldie—Henry King's *Jesse James* which came some eleven years later. No one could call this a classic but it was fair entertainment, well photographed, and marked by the interesting study by Henry Fonda of Frank James.

Tyrone Power, on the other hand—another bit of unfortunate casting due to the star system prevailing—glamorized Jesse beyond all belief. Nothing in James' record shows that he was other than a calculating Bad 'Un, even though the badness might have been bred of war.

Real life town marshals—or rather, one particular town marshal, Wyatt Earp—come off better.

Earp, born Wyatt Berry Stapp Earp, in 1848, was a lawman in the Kansas cowtowns who gravitated from Wichita to Dodge City, where he was assistant marshal, and then went on to Tombstone, a mining town in Arizona.

Here his brother, Virgil Walter Earp, was city marshal, and here it was that the incident that perhaps, above all, sums up the law and order issue of those times and which has certainly been commemorated over all other incidents, took place on October 26, 1881. Legend knows it—and legend has certainly left its mark on it—as the Gunfight of the O.K. Corral.

The bare facts are that Wyatt, Virgil and another brother (Morgan), aided by John Henry Holliday, a dentist who had become a gunman, took on a local ruffian named Ike Clanton, his son Billy, and Frank and Tom McLaury, and dispatched the two McLaurys and Billy.

Later, Virgil was seriously wounded and Morgan assassinated. Wyatt and another brother (Warren) went after the killers and got three of them. Not

surprisingly, the Earps then turned their backs on Tombstone. They had surely underscored the name. Subsequently Wyatt gambled his way round the mining camps (it was a recognized and respected way of earning a living) and turned up, strangely enough, in 1896, as referee of the world heavyweight boxing championship between Bob Fitzsimmons and Tom Sharkey.

He was a thoroughly respectable and affluent citizen in his later days and lived on to the good age, considering his early circumstances, of 71.

Law and Order (1932), a film starring Walter Huston and Harry Carey, had blazed the Earp screen trail with a gritty version of the O.K. Corral happenings, although the true-life characters were never named. *Frontier Marshal* (1939) starring Randolph Scott and *Wichita* (1955, Joel McCrea) also told the story.

To most modern cinemagoers, however, the Corral incident and the confused events and motivations which led to it have been best served by two films, John Ford's *My Darling Clementine* and John Sturges' *Gunfight at the O.K. Corral* (1957).

Ford makes much of the visit of a lovely named Clementine (Cathy Downs) searching for her presumably long-lost love, none other than the gun-notorious Doc Holliday, now, alas devoted to the bottle and in the latter stages of tuberculosis.

The consumptive hero/heroine burning a brief candle at both ends while life still lasts is one of the standbys of empurpled romantic fiction and in this instance we have Victor Mature breathing fire and fury at the slightest hint of an insult before breathing more heavily into his handkerchief. He's a touchy character and, on the whole, not overplayed, although some critics have thought so.

Earp (Henry Fonda deliciously *under*playing) finds him touchy but nevertheless strikes up an understanding which one feels will blossom into grudging joint gun-action should the need arise. The need is obviously there in villainous Old Man Clanton (Walter Brennan) and his infamous viper's nest of sons.

There is deviation on the way, a revenge motive attributed to Fonda, and the jealous intervention of a dancing girl (Linda Darnell) but the path is well and truly pointed to that rendezvous at the Corral.

The facts don't really bear a lot of scrutiny although Ford has been said to have got them direct from Earp—at least the 'battle' facts—whom he got to know in his younger days in movies. But Earp, it should be remembered, had

LEFT *Kirk Douglas as Doc Holliday in John Sturges'* Gunfight at the OK
Corral *(Paramount 1957)*.
ABOVE *Randolph Scott in* Frontier Marshal *(20th Century Fox 1939)*.

no great reputation for 'straight talking'. Most of
these men lovingly fondled and enlarged the
legend.

The action is crisp, nicely photographed and the
story well told. But we always remember *My
Darling Clementine* for its other qualities—for the
leisurely lulls and the 'time off' taken on the way.
This is Ford indulging himself, as was his wont,
but on this occasion the indulgences all come off
and are tinged with magic.

It's a film of touches—Fonda, seated, adjusting
his boots and his balance while the world, such as
it is, goes by; Fonda, the peacemaker, right-and-
properly in church; Fonda, with an olde-worlde
frontier concept of courtesy leading his lady in the
out of doors dance.

Pure magic. But was Earp such a man? It's
doubtful.

Burt Lancaster plays the part in *Gunfight at the
O.K. Corral*, with Kirk Douglas as Doc.

Here much effort is spent in establishing and
developing the relationship—Wyatt and Virgil
meet in Texas and meet again in Dodge City to
share adventures of a double-edged nature before
the scene finally shifts to Tombstone in preparation
for what the title promises.

It's a film that has some of the Sturges virtues,
but not all. It doesn't however disappoint when it
comes to the crunch—the gunfight itself. This is
magnificently staged. It probably equals anything
that law and order movies have produced in set-
piece battles. It is reputed to have taken four days
to shoot, working at it eleven hours a day—a lot of
time and serious attention for what the historians
tell us, in actual fact, took some 32 seconds. But
that's movies. How could any audience be content
with such a brisk shoot-up when legend spoke of
a full-blown battle?

It's all summed up in the succinct piece of advice
given by veteran newspaperman Dutton Peabody
in the closing bits of *The Man Who Shot Liberty
Valance.*

Quoth Peabody, knowing old man of the West:
'When the legend becomes fact—print the legend!'

The Westerners

THE customary round-up of faithful workers in the cause of the Western becomes an entirely different matter in a book of this sort which is concerned with outstanding examples of the genre. From this point of view a long service medal doesn't necessarily commend itself as a virtue. A distinguished service medal seems more apposite.

This is not arbitrarily a disparagement of players and their talents. They can be the victims, like all of us, of the vagaries of time, luck and circumstances. As with the mysterious stranger riding into town, they have to be at the right place at the right time if they are going to make it in the great movie.

Take, for instance, the case of Joel McCrea and Randolph Scott. Nothing this pair of sound performers have done during their long Western service equals their late gallop for Sam Peckinpah in his wonderful *Ride The High Country* (*Guns in the Afternoon*, in Britain) (1962). And that's not forgetting that Scott has done some interesting things with director Budd Boetticher.

On the other hand, many directors and players have looked into the Western scene only briefly and departed, having made sure of their niche in the gallery of great Western movies. Whereas some worthy and devoted practitioners may have finished up saddle-sore and weary with no luck at all.

Two typical scenes from a Bud Boetticher film—Randolph Scott in
Decision at Sundown *(Brown-Scott 1957).*

The fact is that the Western is an almost obligatory test-piece for the topline American actor or director. It's a matter of professional comparison and pride—it's a bit like brilliant British actors matching their Hamlets.

And it's a fact, also, that for a long time the Western in all its shapes and forms was a steady way of making a living. You could more or less make a career of it without getting starry-eyed about your 'art'.

Long service plus the distinguished result is therefore a rarity. But it can happen. . . .

John (Duke) Wayne would today be reckoned the prime example. The record speaks for itself: *Stagecoach*, *Fort Apache*, *Red River*, *She Wore a Yellow Ribbon*, *Rio Grande*, *The Searchers*, *Rio Bravo*, *The Man Who Shot Liberty Valance*.

A man could surely rest on that. It's an astonishing roll-call, all the starry way from *The Big Trail* to *True Grit* (1968) and beyond.

Wayne always had certain things going for him—chiefly his long association with director John Ford. But there were other things going against him—his relegation into the second league (of 'B' pictures) following *The Big Trail*; the extra-ordinary and unperceptive denigration he suffered for so long. Few actors have been so underrated. His limitations may be obvious, but within his range—and this is particularly true of the limits set by a Western—he has rare gifts, not only of conveying character but the feel of the time and the place and the *kind* of people that the time and place created. This is perhaps best pointed in the Ethan character who dominates *The Searchers*. You feel that Ethan couldn't have belonged at any other time or place. He was moulded by territory and experience.

All this comes from conviction. Wayne is a 'feeling' man, where the West is concerned. It means a lot to him—the whole experience, its beliefs, its very flavour. Somewhere lodged within him is a bit of the old West and this is the inner strength he draws on.

Wayne began as Marion Michael Morrison—born to a Winterset (Iowa) apothecary, on May 26, 1907. There was Scots-Irish blood in his veins. The family moved west to the edge of the Mojave Desert, California, when Marion was about seven years old and for a while led a homesteading life, before they moved on again to Glendale where

BELOW *An unusual stick-up for 'Big John' in George Sherman's* Big Jake *(Batjac 1971)*.
RIGHT *'Big John' strolls through Mark Rydell's* The Cowboys *(Sanford/WB 1971)*.
OVERLEAF Firecreek *(WB/Seven Arts 1967) carried a full complement of Westerners. The cast included James Stewart, Henry Fonda, Dean Jagger and Jack Elam.*

LEFT *Gregory Peck notched up another Western on his gun belt in* Mackenna's Gold *(Highroad/Columbia 1968) and Omar Sharif made a rare appearance.*
ABOVE *John Wayne starred with Ann-Margret and Rod Taylor in* The Train Robbers *(Batjac 1973).*
BELOW *'Duke' at last won an Oscar for his portrayal of a fat, old, eye-patched lawman in* True Grit *(Paramount 1969), here seen with his co-star the ebullient Miss Kim Darby.*

Doc Morrison went back to his old line of business.

It was here that the young Morrison got his soubriquet 'Duke'—from a large Airedale dog he parked at the fire station while he was at school. Tall and ruggedly handsome, young Duke grew up into a nineteen-twenties version of the All American Boy. He won a football scholarship to the University of Southern California, where one of the ways he saw himself through college was to sell tickets to well-breeched fans.

He got into pictures, and thereby into Westerns, strangely enough by doing a 'ticket favour' for the greatest Western star of the twenties—Tom Mix.

Mix helped him get a vacation job in the movies. At first it was moving props for a John Ford picture. Ford came across Wayne rounding up

ABOVE *The young Gary Cooper in Victor Fleming's* The Virginian *(Paramount 1929).*
RIGHT *Gary Cooper in Anthony Mann's* Man of the West *(Ashton 1958).*

geese that had strayed on to the set. Ford himself had started as a prop boy. He teased Wayne about the geese, challenged him about his football, and that was the start. There were a lot of props still to be shifted before the big football player even became 'bit' player—but from such small, strange, luck-ridden beginnings towering achievement *can* eventually grow.

Gary Cooper was another who served long and loyally—he was an extra in silent Westerns and then a star. There was *The Virginian* (1929) and *The Westerner* (1940) in which Walter Brennan put in such a wonderful performance as Judge Roy Bean. And, of course, there had been the plum role of Wild Bill Hickok in *The Plainsman* and, way back, a good part in *The Winning of Barbara Worth* that had really got him going.

But Cooper's niche really depends upon Will Kane in *High Noon*. That is, unless room is found for an excellent Anthony Mann movie, *Man of the West* (1958). Such was the aura of this man and such the general belief that this was the look, the

voice, the walk of the West, that in our celestial movie show, a Cooper movie would be a necessity.

Cooper, born in 1901, in Montana, came of British origins. His father had left England when he was 19 and he subsequently married a girl from Kent.

The young Cooper, christened Frank James, had an early ranching background, since his father owned 600 Montana acres, but he was to return to England where he went to his father's old school in Dunstable.

World War One, however, saw him back in Montana and here Gary was to get the ranching and riding experience and general Western know-how that was to make him look so right in all his Western movies.

He was gifted as an artist, particularly as a cartoonist, but got little commercial encouragement and drifted, like so many Western players, into 'extra' work. He had built up a great deal of Western experience as an extra before he finally got his chance in *The Winning of Barbara Worth*.

RIGHT *Marlene Dietrich and Una Merkel in one of the most uproariously funny fight scenes in all Westerns—their saloon bar battle in* Destry Rides Again *(Universal 1939).*
ABOVE *James Stewart tries cooling down the girls and then fends off Dietrich (*above right*).*

James Stewart came rather late in the day to Westerns. He has said that they were helpful at a somewhat difficult point of his career. It seems hard to imagine how anything could ever have been difficult for this universally popular actor with a range and record of 'big' films probably beyond compare.

Mr. Smith Goes To Washington, The Philadelphia Story, The Glenn Miller Story, The Man Who Shot Liberty Valance—it's a wide range of subjects and styles.

And yet it could be truthfully said that the Western suits him as well as any. He has an affection for it and pride in it that shine through every part. He also has quite unusual diligence and dedication. For instance, he showed intense interest and took great care about the technical side of the firearm in question when making *Winchester '73* (1950) for Anthony Mann.

Stewart is assured of his place in the pantheon for his out-of-step Indian sympathizer in *Broken Arrow* and his pushing lawyer in the Liberty Valance picture. But he has given other notable performances. He starred opposite Marlene Dietrich in George Marshall's comedy Western *Destry Rides Again* (1939) and in other Mann movies of distinction—such as *The Naked Spur* (1953) and *The Man From Laramie* (1955).

Universal Film S.A
présente une production
JOE PASTERNAK
interprétée par

DIETRICH & *James* **STEWART**
Marlène

FEMME *ou*
démon

(DESTRY RIDES AGAIN)

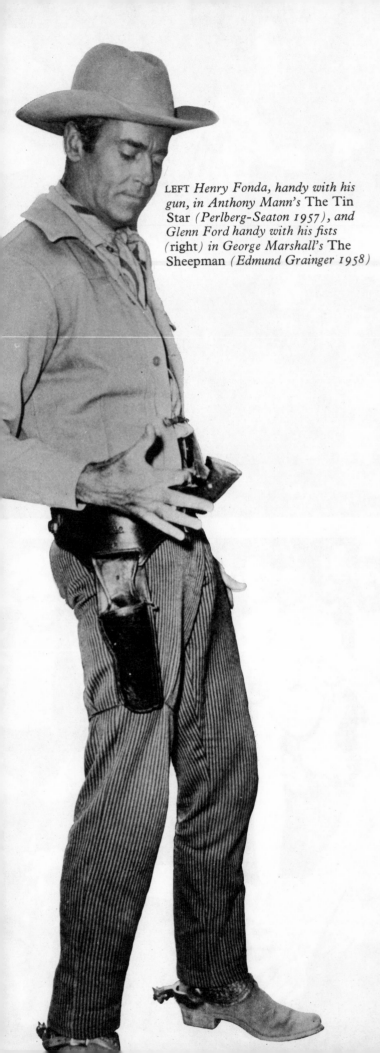

LEFT *Henry Fonda, handy with his gun, in Anthony Mann's* The Tin Star *(Perlberg-Seaton 1957), and Glenn Ford handy with his fists (*right*) in George Marshall's* The Sheepman *(Edmund Grainger 1958)*

The contribution made by Henry Fonda to quality Westerns is often overlooked. He made his point early with *The Oxbow Incident.* (*Drums Along The Mohawk*, 1939, a Ford picture about late 18th century pioneering in the Mohawk Valley, doesn't qualify as a Western in classic 'time' terms but it had already marked out Fonda's potent presence in Western-type roles.)

Fonda's Wyatt Earp in *My Darling Clementine* secured his place among the immortals, but there has been other fine work—the stubborn, mistaken cavalry officer in *Fort Apache*, the subtly-played gunfighter in *Warlock*, and the gunman-tutor in Mann's *The Tin Star* (1957).

Glenn Ford, another subtle performer, staked his claim with two films that were largely ignored when they were released but are now ranked among the best of their particular kinds—Delmer Daves' *3.10 To Yuma* (1957), a close-textured psychological drama, and George Marshall's *The Sheepman* (1958), arguably the best comedy Western ever made. Van Heflin can also point to *3.10 To Yuma* and make an even stronger claim—his enduring sod-buster in *Shane*.

Kirk Douglas, the great all-rounder? Certainly with *Gunfight at O.K. Corral* and also with David Miller's *Lonely are the Brave* (1962), in the opinion of many his greatest performance.

Durable but also distinguished service becomes a much simpler matter when it comes to discussing the 'other ranks'— the supporting actors, second unit directors and so on.

Where would the Western be without them—the faces villainous, cowardly, pathetic and humorous that fill in those parts of the screen away from the star, his well-billed adversary, his horse or his inamorata of the moment?

Some cinemagoers say they derive their main pleasure in a Western from its detail. They tend to look upon the screen as a canvas and dwell upon the chiaroscuro, the telling bits and pieces—the way a shadow falls hard and long from an evening-shot cactus; the way a poke bonnet is framed and somehow blessed by a wagon wheel; how a little dance of dust heralds a stagecoach in long-shot.

They are the kind of people who pay second and even third visits to *Shane* and *The Searchers* and make each visit an occasion of fresh discovery. And they are expressing a proper kind of appreciation. But the human detail that contributes to the whole is just as important. So all honour to those who have consistently supplied it. Some like Lee Marvin, most dynamic and impressive 'heavy' over the years, have gone on to more important

ABOVE *A* Wild Bunch *(WB/Seven Arts 1969) line-up—Ben Johnson, Warren Oates, William Holden, Ernest Borgnine.*

roles. Others have slid up and down the 'import- ance' scale. And, yet again, there are those who have kept their place, a respected one, faithfully and accurately filling in the background.

First thoughts go to the John Ford supporters, such as Ward Bond, Harry Carey Jun., Ben Johnson, Victor McLaglen, whose contribution to the cavalry trilogy has already been noted.

Johnson, the former Oklahoma-born horse wrangler, 'supported' for Ford in *She Wore a Yellow Ribbon, Rio Grande* and *Cheyenne Autumn* and co-starred with Harry Carey Jun. in *Wagon- master.* But also he enhanced three other notable Western movies—*Shane,* Sam Pekinpah's *The Wild Bunch* (1968) and Marlon Brando's interesting *One Eyed Jacks.* It is an extraordinary record that is sometimes overlooked.

Carey, himself son of an old silent Western star, can point to some almost equally distinguished service. Among his Ford Westerns, and apart from his joint-starring role in *Wagonmaster,* were *She Wore a Yellow Ribbon* and *Rio Grande, The Searchers* and *Cheyenne Autumn.* He also appeared in Hawks' *Rio Bravo* and Hathaway's *From Hell to Texas* (1958).

The late Ward Bond, who was to blossom into a popular T.V. Western star, had Ford appearances in *My Darling Clementine, Fort Apache, Wagon- master* and *The Searchers.*

Another member of the John Ford Rolling Stock Company, although not strictly an actor— rather a great all-round supporter—was Yakima Canutt, possibly the greatest Western stunt man of all time, and a brilliant initiator and organizer of action sequences. Canutt, who had been a silent star, is perhaps best known to Western fans as the man who packed the thrills into that imperishable and much borrowed and copied chase sequence in *Stagecoach.*

What about the old-timers—the bristly grouches and cracker-barrel philosophers who enliven and enrich the Western way?

One name comes foremost, that of Walter Brennan, who won an Academy Award for the best supporting player as long ago as 1940 for his Judge Roy Bean in the Gary Cooper picture, *The Westerner.* He has three awards in all.

Brennan added his own kind of distinction to three highly distinguished films. He was John Wayne's 'pardner' in *Red River;* Stumpy, the crippled jailer who lent a different sort of aid to Wayne in *Rio Bravo;* and the not-so-amusing Old Man Clanton in *My Darling Clementine.*

Edgar Buchanan also ranks high for his work in this particular field. *Shane, Ride the High Country, The Sheepman*—he's up there alongside Brennan.

And, when it comes to villains, who so downright successfully villainous (Marvin notwithstanding)

as Lee Van Cleef (*Gunfight at O.K. Corral*, *The Man Who Shot Liberty Valance*) and not forgetting King Vidor's *Man Without a Star* (1955) and Mann's *The Tin Star*? Van Cleef has gone on—one won't say progressed—to star in Spaghetti Westerns.

The late, lamented John Ford always seemed indifferent to critical acclaim, invariably giving the impression that he was just doing a job and the job was mainly Western movies. If anything he seemed bored with the appraisal heaped upon him through the years. But the fact remains that no director can equal his record—a substantial body of work, most of it of the highest quality.

Ford talked rarely about his work and even then in the most laconic throwaway idiom. He was old-fashioned enough to believe that an artist's work should speak for itself. He probably wouldn't have used the word 'artist'—he might have settled for craftsman—but few would disagree that, in the best of Ford, art in the Western movie gets its finest flowering. This is certainly so in purely romantic terms.

Perhaps he was wise to keep comparatively silent. For he was an intuitive artist and knew as such he was part and parcel of a mystery. The magic just happens. Craft and experience can prepare the way but from then on it's up to the gods.

James Stewart, in an interview, once ascribed all the best moments in cinema—the truly magic moments—to 'accident'. Describing how John Ford worked he gave it a phrase—'planned inspiration'. The master, he implied, had a mysterious way of working, his wonders to perform. 'He knows camera,' he said, 'and he knows

ABOVE *Glenn Ford among the girls in* The Sheepman *(Edmund Grainger 1958)*.
BELOW *Lee Van Cleef and Stephen Boyd in Henry King's* The Bravados *(20th Century Fox 1958)*.

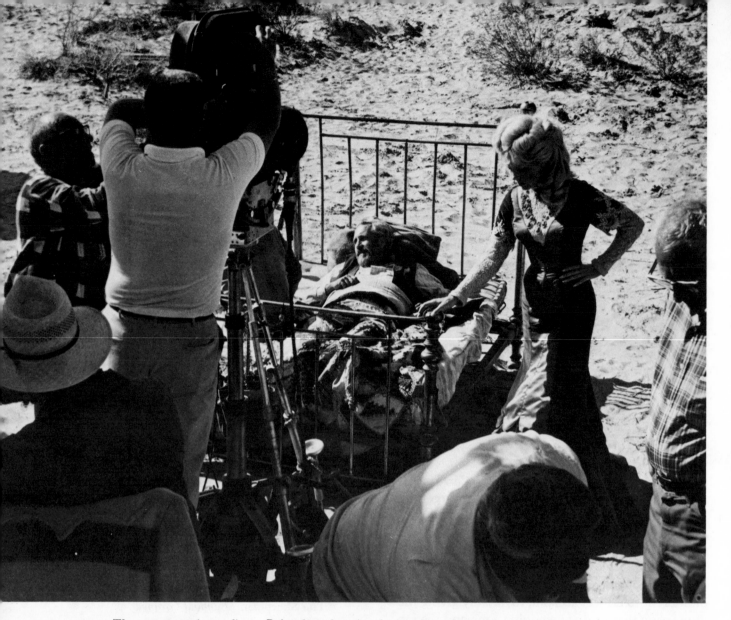

The camera trains on Jason Robards on location during the making of
The Ballad of Cable Hogue *(WB 1970).*

composition, but he keeps actors from knowing *exactly* what is going to happen next.'

So we have the picture of a man, patiently waiting for an 'accident', the word Ford would probably have preferred to the more pretentious 'inspiration'.

'He knows composition'. . . .

It's immediately apparent, for of all his gifts—story-teller, poet, off and on humorist, landscape painter—the last talent impresses most. This is logical, for he once said that as a child he had painting aspirations and that perhaps an eye for composition was the only attribute he had brought to movie-making.

The name Ford was born with was Sean Aloysius O'Feeney, which explains a lot—the characters with Irish origins who flit in and out of his Westerns, and a certain style of humour. He

was born in Maine in 1895 and after leaving Portland High School in 1913 went to Hollywood where his brother Francis was already engaged in film-making.

His brother was then known as 'Ford' and Sean was to adopt this surname. He was known as Jack rather than John in those days.

John Ford started at the bottom in Universal's studios—doing odd jobs, then graduating to prop boy and later assistant-director. It could also be said that he started right at the bottom as far as Westerns were concerned. For his early work was with Westerns. He made them with Harry Carey principally, but also worked with Tom Mix and Hoot Gibson. His breakthrough picture was the railroad epic *The Iron Horse* which came in 1924.

For all his reputation as an artist Ford was not known as a 'fancy shot' director. He panned sparingly, normally, only when the action made this an absolute demand. He was reported as once laying down the axiom: 'Nail down your camera!'

His weaknesses have been described as an over-indulgence in the sentimental and in knockabout comedy. But such 'weaknesses' could become virtues when he was working at his best. For 'sentimentality' read good honest sentiment and for 'knockabout' a real, salty, ironic suggestion of the contrasts of frontier life. He was an artist with profound feeling for time and place and people. If John Wayne is the leathery face of the legend John Ford was the man in love with it.

Who is the most promising contender for his title? Surely Sam Peckinpah. This is another director whose work is charged with feeling, although of a different kind and with different motivations. The best is possibly still to come from Peckinpah and yet he has already staked his claim with four fine offerings—*Ride the High Country*, *The Wild Bunch*, *The Ballad of Cable Hogue* (1970) and *Pat Garrett and Billy the Kid*.

The first three pictures are of an 'off the beaten trail' kind which, with others, will be discussed later.

Some directors work from the point of an entirely different concept. John Sturges for example gives a cool look to his people and their predicaments. He often keeps his players at a distance, showing them in long-shot against all that is harsh, unfeeling and hostile in their bit of territory. Sometimes this gives the effect of classical tragedy and its inevitability. The Western Fates, one feels, are brooding over the characters, unmoved and immovable.

Sturges has given us *Gunfight at O.K. Corral*, a 'contemporary' Western, *Bad Day at Black Rock* (1954) and *The Magnificent Seven*.

Howard Hawks has ranged in his time (he was born in 1896 and was directing as long ago as 1926) over the whole spectrum of cinema and in almost every form he has tackled he has achieved popular success and a varying degree of artistic appreciation. *Red River* and *Rio Bravo* are his lasting testament as far as Westerns are concerned and no one could deny that he has made an eminent contribution. Two other veterans earn our gratitude. *The Gunfighter* ranks as probably the best film ever made by Henry King, a director of over 100 films, made in the span of 45 years. Henry Hathaway who began directing in 1933 had a late Western flowering with *From Hell to Texas* (*Manhunt*, in Britain) (1958), which had little acclaim at the time, and, in 1968, the much loved

True Grit, for which the aged and eye-patched John Wayne at last got an Oscar.

Delmer Daves isn't quite such a veteran but he was working in films as long ago as the early 1920s—attending to props when they were making the first screen epic, *The Covered Wagon*.

Daves lived for a while in his youth among Indians and this probably explains his Indian-sympathetic *Broken Arrow*, also his attention for accuracy in Western detail—Bill Hart would have applauded him for this. *3.10 To Yuma*, his Glenn Ford and Van Heflin classic suspense story, a film in quite a different vein, is his other major contribution.

Cults tend to crystallize around directors from time to time and this has certainly been the case with two of the most recently publicized—Budd Boetticher and the late Anthony Mann.

Mann's work is full of the intensities and passions of his people—not to mention the odd obsession. It is visually dramatic—the action is always excitingly photographed—but thereafter, particularly in certain sequences, it tends to be a matter of taste. Dialogue at times has its banalities and out and out melodrama isn't far around the corner. But mainly because of his settings and his photography and the sheer dynamic impetus of his storytelling and the intensity of his people, most of these high-powered films carry conviction.

Following their *Winchester '73* Anthony Mann made a string of films with James Stewart, in which the normally casual-styled actor was required to work up an unwonted degree of near-hysteria and did so extraordinarily well. Mann's outstanding film, though, was *Man of the West*, starring Gary Cooper.

Budd Boetticher has also received much attention. To some extent this is merited—particularly for the example offered of how a high level of excellence can be obtained and maintained, working on a modest budget and within a small canvas.

Boetticher used the veteran Randolph Scott as the keystone of his run of best pictures, beginning with *The Tall T* (1958), and including *Decision at Sundown* (1957), *Buchanan Rides Alone* (1958) and *Comanche Station* (1960).

The central figure, played by Scott in these films, is essentially what is known in 'literary jargon' as a Hemingway character—a stoical 'hero' going his own way, come what may, remaining true to his code even to the death.

Perhaps this isn't surprising when one learns that Budd is a fervent bull-fighting afficionado—as was Ernest, before him.

Off the Beaten Trail

SOME Westerns don't conform. They are either outside the recognized period or have preoccupations of their own, other than the traditional historic issues. Yet some of these films are so intrinsically Western in 'feel' and attain such stature that only a stickler well on the way to becoming a bigot would keep them off his favoured list. On the other hand there are films using the Western form whose preoccupations, or, in their case, perhaps 'motives' is a better word, seem suspect. King Vidor's *Duel in the Sun*, a 1945 picture, a triangle drama involving two brothers (Gregory Peck and Joseph Cotten) and a sultry half-breed (Jennifer Jones) comes immediately to mind. It invariably leaves an after-taste of conscious exploitation—'Why not pump sex into the Western and see what we've got?' What they got, in fact, was a top-heavy piece of deep purple, laughable at times, which quite overpowered some likely action aspects.

Now and again a film pops up which is right out of period but is somehow more Western in classic terms than many an offering lodged securely in the 1870s or early 1880s.

LEFT *King Vidor's busty* Duel in the Sun *(Selznick/Selznick Int. 1946)*. BELOW *Horst Buchholz having woman trouble in* The Magnificent Seven *(Mirisch-Alpha 1960)*.

Take the astonishing case of John Sturges' *Bad Day at Black Rock* (1954). This fine film is set in post-World War Two times, but shift a railway track, knock down a gas station, and in no time at all you're back some seventy odd years. It's the same pathetic little township, not noticeably more handsome than that huddle of buildings, that early eyesore of ribbon development in *Shane*. It's stuck out, lost and forlorn somewhere in the desert, baking under a blazing, indifferent sky. It's festering with a sore of guilt and is entirely lacking in any sense of civic pride and purpose. It's under the thrall of a tyrannical boss-man (Robert Ryan) and his prime 'heavy' (Ernest Borgnine). And the local citizenry are traditionally cowed—not excluding the sheriff (Dean Jagger), who furtively seeks traditional solace, out of a bottle.

In fact, the town's just waiting for the mysterious stranger to come riding in, clean things up, set everything on a more hopeful footing, and then ride away.

He arrives, sure enough, in the person of a one-armed Spencer Tracy who gets off a streamlined train which normally wouldn't think of stopping at such a God-forsaken dump. But Tracy, you feel at once, might just as easily be accommodating a horse in the livery stables or securing it to a hitching post outside a saloon. Western identification is immediate and you wonder what the trick is.

Perhaps only in retrospect does it become apparent. It's played that way right from the start. Could it, in fact, given the scene, the situation and the people, be played any other way? You can almost hear Tracy, Ryan and co. agreeing: 'Well, this is a Western so let's forget this stuff,' meaning the railway, the gas station and the jeep around the corner, before slipping on their parts like well-worn clothes.

And thereafter it's all a matter of style—the provocative banter in the bar, the slow-burn build up of tension, the isolation of the intruding stranger, the flaring of action (Tracy's one-armed, unarmed combat techniques taming the bull-like Borgnine). All this is in keeping with the way it has been handled so often before.

Sturges imposes the mood in his shots, setting man, as ever, against Western environment, making it all as stark and dramatic as that unequivocal title.

Bad Day at Black Rock also ranks as a distinguished suspense film. The stranger, in this case, has come on a mission and both audience and townsfolk have to learn by degrees what he's about. But the guilty always have a pretty shrewd suspicion. After all, the life they all lead is a conspiracy of silence—ever since the day when, topped up with too much 'patriotism' or, rather, making it the excuse for evil tendencies, they did something dreadful to a fellow citizen of Japanese origins.

The stranger, naturally, sorts it all out and by the time he rides out of town—on the streamliner—the implication is that he has returned to the citizens their civic soul and sense of purpose. As in—well, so many traditional Westerns come to mind.

Impact, style and suspense—yes, *Bad Day at Black Rock* has all these ingredients in good measure. But there is another element that finally lends it its special distinction. This is the Spencer Tracy characterization. It not only has depth—it carries with it the suggestion of hidden depths. We want to know more and more about this stranger—more, in fact, than the film will allow us to know.

It is interesting to compare the steely resilience of Tracy in this picture with another tough character (a domineering father) he played in Dmytryk's *Broken Lance* (1954), adapted from a non-Western, *House of Strangers*. His playing in *Bad Day at Black Rock*, despite the hairiness of the character, is illumined with real feeling—in fact, all sorts of hinted feelings. Somehow this is missing in *Broken Lance* where the domineering Dad seems so synthetic, a criticism that can be levelled against the film itself.

John Huston's *The Treasure of the Sierra Madre* (1948) is very different stuff. It's a controversial choice of a Western even in this elastic category, although its 'Western elements' are usually admitted.

It is set in Mexico and the year is 1920. A shifty-eyed tramp (Humphrey Bogart) and his sidekick

LEFT *Jennifer Jones in* Duel in the Sun *(Selznick/Selznick Int. 1946)*.
BELOW *Spencer Tracy seen here with Robert Wagner, Hugh O'Brian and Richard Widmark in Edward Dmytryk's not wholly successful* Broken Lance *(20th Century Fox 1954)*.

ABOVE *Tim Holt and Humphrey Bogart in John Huston's* The Treasure of the Sierra Madre *(WB-First National 1948).*
RIGHT *Edward G. Robinson in J. Lee Thompson's rumbustious, tongue-in-cheek* Mackenna's Gold *(Highroad/Columbia 1968).*
OVERLEAF *Raymond Massey (*left*) and Gregory Peck (*right*) seemed larger than life in* Mackenna's Gold *(Highroad/Columbia 1968).*

(Tim Holt son of the old silent star, Jack Holt) listen in a dosshouse to the ramblings of another wanderer—an old-timer, played by Walter Huston.

The old man goes on and on about gold, although leavening his love for prospecting with seemingly out-of-character warnings about what the lust for gold can do to a man.

Bogart wins money in a lottery and all three of them decide to mount an expedition to the mountains. Surviving an attack by bandits led by a villainous Mexican whose title is Goldhat (symbolic?) and played by Alfonso Bedoya, the tramps at last get down to prospecting with fair results.

From then on the film becomes a parable, justifying all the old-timer's dosshouse warnings. Love of gold begins whittling away at whatever moral fibre this unlikely trio ever possessed. The Bogart character suffers the most. Always faintly unpleasant he now becomes a deranged and

febrile monster. Anyone who comes between him and sole-ownership of the gold-dust hoard gets short shrift. First to go is a stranger (Bruce Bennett) who tries to get in on the act. Even the pardnerties of loyalty are finally broken.

Goldhat haunts the whole enterprise and it is he who catches up with Bogart, when the madman, as he certainly is now, thinks he has done for the rest. The bandits smile their oleaginous smiles, sever the traveller from all earthly yearnings, appraise the value of his mules and apparel—and those little bags the mules are carrying? Who wants those?

They're tossed away.

It's a grimly ironic film—perhaps the irony is too consciously hammered home. For Goldhat and his crowd also get their come-uppance and the other two pardners who have now caught up with things can retrieve nothing from the situation.

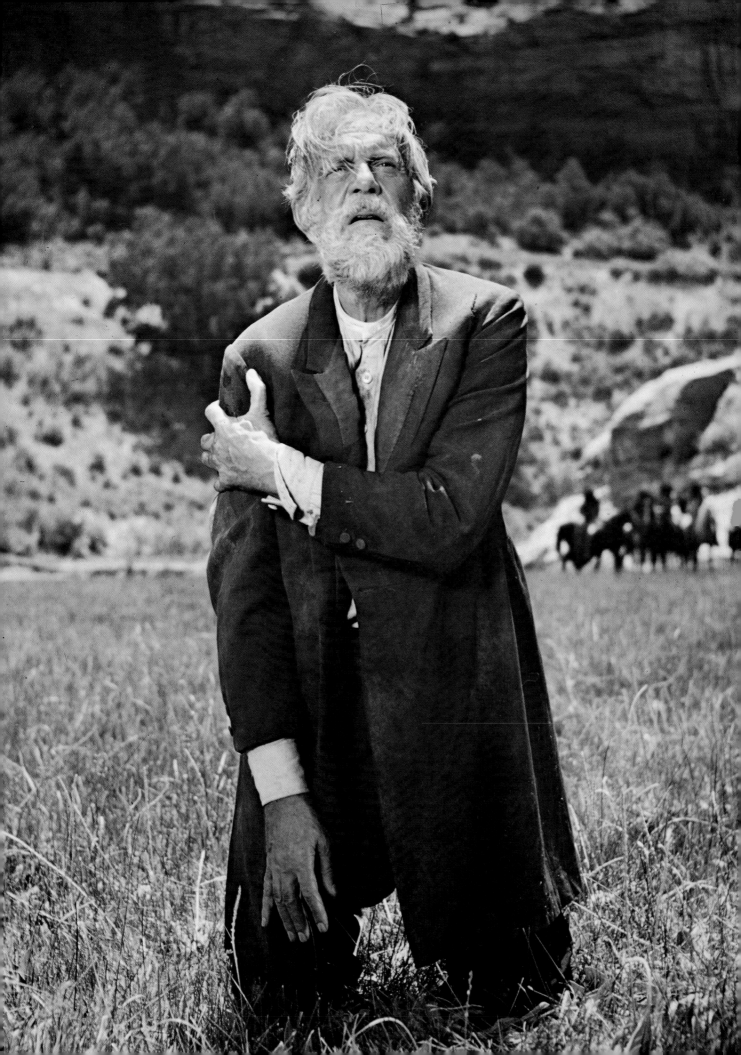

They look around for the missing bags but the precious dust, alas, now keeps company with ordinary dust.

Huston has managed it all magnificently. It is a remarkable film however categorized. There are vividly photographed scenes with Indians in the mountains and holding a celebratory fiesta after the old-timer has cured an Indian child, and a magnificent last stage tableau where the bandits seem to savour with showmanship their farewells to an easy come-easy go world.

It is vivid, too, in the performances. Bogart with his temperature always climbing with gold-fever. The director's father and celebrated actor, Walter, as the old timer, concurring in his way with the bandit philosophy—what will be, will be, but it's no crying matter.

But the real significance of *The Treasure of the Sierra Madre* in the context of the Western film is its seminal subtle influence on the genre. Echoes of it constantly sound in Westerns firmly sited in the traditional period. Touches give nagging reminders.

Huston's way with the Indians and the bandits, and with the Bogart character, strike off flashes. One would particularly say this was the case with Sam Peckinpah. Even with the detail of dwindling returns—the dust to dust ironic denouement—well, one remembers what happened to the loot in the enjoyable John Wayne, Kirk Douglas movie *The War Wagon* (1967), and the dollar bill paper-chase that mortified Paul Newman and Robert

LEFT *Indian defiance in* Soldier Blue *(Avco-Embassy 1970)*.
ABOVE *and* BELOW *Two scenes from* The War Wagon *(Batjac for Universal 1967), Burt Kennedy's exciting and ingenious Western adventure film, starring John Wayne and Kirk Douglas.*

ABOVE *Paul Newman and Robert Redford teamed up for one of the best Western relationships ever in George Roy Hill's* Butch Cassidy and the Sundance Kid *(Campanile/20th Century Fox/Newman-Foreman 1969)*.
ABOVE RIGHT *Kirk Douglas in a contemporary Western,* Lonely are the Brave *(Universal-International/Joel 1955)*.
BELOW RIGHT *Kirk Douglas again, this time in King Vidor's range war melodrama* Man without a Star *(Universal-Int. 1955)*.

Redford ('Think you used enough dynamite, there, Butch?') in *Butch Cassidy and the Sundance Kid*.

The shadow of a helicopter looms over *Lonely are the Brave*, so no Western could be more out of time-scale than this one, and yet, paradoxically, no central character was ever more truly Western than Jack Burns, the strange wanderer, played by Kirk Douglas.

Douglas in this film version of Edward Abbey's moving novel *Brave Cowboy*—the excellent script was the work of Dalton Trumbo—is, among a number of other things, a man who hates barbed wire. He showed a similar distaste for it in King Vidor's *Man Without a Star* (1955), which was a traditional cattle range rumpus movie, and in those circumstances that seemed reasonable enough. But *Lonely are the Brave* is a film set in the New Mexico of 1953 and such behaviour now seems totally irrational.

But then he's an irrational, quite extraordinary man. He rides a horse called Whisky when the world flashes past him in Cadillacs. He carries a guitar and sings folksy ballads of the old West. Arriving in the concrete of Duke City he is quite confident that in order to free a pal he has only got to break into jail, fool a sheriff and make his getaway. After all, it's Western territory and this was always the way of it.

Who and what is he? The question bears examination for he is one of the most intriguing characters in the whole Western portrait gallery. He is never really explained in the book, nor indeed in the film. He is drawn and stated and the rest is left to the reader or audience. You watch the way he moves, you listen to what he says and the way he says it. You observe his strange actions and reactions. But mostly you are left to make your own conclusions.

Two scenes from Lonely are the Brave *(Universal-Int./Joel 1955), in which, in the opinion of many critics, Kirk Douglas gave the outstanding performance of his long career.*

Is it a case of a fantasist totally hooked on the Western legend? Has he seen too many Western movies (probably 'B' features)? Has he read too much Western pulp fiction? Is he so bemused by it all that he is incapable of realizing that the world has moved on, is running out of grass, or tolerance for oddballs with a preference for grass?

Is he making a protest about what the West has become, and is seeking, in his inarticulate way, after different values? Is he just pure throwback, a man belonging to another time? This figures, as he might say. He would belong so splendidly, with his simple values.

Whatever he is, he's a profoundly tragic conception. . . .

The old friend he is there to aid (Michael Kane) has been jailed for giving shelter to over-the-border illegal immigrants. Douglas calls on his buddy's wife, sensitively played by Gena Rowlands, who seems as touched and bemused by him as anyone in the audience. In order to get Kane out of prison he decides that he first needs to get into it

himself and so after a saloon bar fight, followed by more fisticuffs at the jail, he gets the cell he wants.

In jail, however, he finds himself once more knocking up against the twentieth century—its mores and inhibitions. The pal doesn't want to conform to the old Western pattern by making a break for it. Far better to serve out his two years and then return to his wife and child knowing that his 'debt to society' has been paid and they will have nothing else to worry about. This is not just pure self-interest. He honestly thinks it the right thing to do.

So having fought his way in, Douglas now has to fight his way out. This he does with the aid of files he brought with him to effect his friend's escape. And out with him go a couple of characters not inhibited by fears and scruples.

So he becomes a man on the run, but, since he still has his horse, an old-style outlaw on the run. There is only time for brief farewells to Gena Rowlands, who obviously dotes on him but thinks him endearingly impossible in 1953, and then he's

heading for the mountains with—naturally—a posse after him.

But no ordinary posse. This is the 20th century version, kitted out with all sorts of technological devices. If this latterday cowboy in his strange, archaic way, is challenging the rule of technology, it is only logical that the long cold arm of science should reach out for him. It does so with walkie-talkie radios, jeeps and even a specially borrowed helicopter.

What chance has he? The sheriff seems puzzled by the situation—that a man on a horse should dare everything against such a formidable array of gadgetry. Since the wanderer is determinedly playing out a Western drama he must inevitably come up against a sheriff and in Walter Matthau he gets him and the film gets just the right degree of counterpoint.

He's an enigmatic man and so everything that comes through him is by inference. And yet it's amazing by a look here and dry remark there, the way he shifts his chewing gum from one cheek to the other, just how much in the way of implied comment does come through.

The sheriff is a man doing a job, without any noticeable relish for the job or, in fact, for anything particularly. He's bored, sceptical, laconic, and you feel that he would like nothing better than for Burns to get out of his territory.

But while the sheriff goes about his manhunting duties in a routine way he lets slip another implication—that deep down in the lethargy and disillusion there's a soft spot for the man on a horse. Is the sheriff at heart—if you could ever find his heart—a bit of a rebel, too?

Despite the odds stacked against him the cowboy reaches the mountain ridge and descends down the other side. Here is the moment of ironic truth. The helicopter and the jeeps and the riflemen have failed to get Jack Burns and Whisky, but they really needn't have bothered. A different bit of technology, an enormous truck, knowing absolutely nothing of the situation, does the job for them—dispassionately and fatally—on Highway 60.

Kirk Douglas loves this picture and has said so. He would probably like to be remembered most of all for his performance as the man out of step, out of his proper time. He most certainly will be and that's not forgetting his dynamic performance in *Champion* (1949), the film that launched him.

His Jack Burns in *Lonely are the Brave* is one of the warmest, most deeply felt characterizations in all Western movies. David Miller directed the film with simplicity and a similar warmth. No more was needed.

Jack Burns was years out of period but there are other characters in Westerns also out of joint and perhaps even more tragically situated.

No dodo was ever more dead than yesterday's hero—many a jaundiced war veteran will testify to this. In fact, the man becomes a relic and a positive embarrassment in the new scene.

Some distinguished Westerns proclaim the fact and their concern is the former heroes ('heroes' in terms of glamour) who are caught up in the turn of the times. These are the men still there in the afterglow period of Western history. It's a long way back now to high noon. The sun of Western derring do has all but left the sky. The last pink light touches ageing, leathery, stubbly faces.

What's to become of them—the men whose day is truly done?

The West is settling down fast. It was always a precipitate settlement once the two railway tracks had joined at Promontory Point. Any violence now in the old style will be in the nature of a last desperate fling. The 20th century and its distinctive perfume of petrol is only just round the corner.

There is nothing to marvel at in the fact that American movies have served this period especially well. Some of the best works in modern American literature get their potency from a built-in elegiac element—a feeling that goes beyond the wistfulness of mere nostalgia, that carries the added depth and dignity of lament.

Sam Peckinpah might be said to have stolen in upon this typically American mood with his *Ride the High Country*, which was filmed in the Mammoth Lake area of California's High Sierras—the first time this area had been used for location work since *Rose Marie*, with Nelson Eddy and Jeanette MacDonald, was made there in 1936. It was not a much-heralded picture but Peckinpah, whose background is the West, gave it a unique quality that soon made it recognized as one of the best Westerns ever made.

It gets additional poignancy from its choice of stars. The two veterans, Joel McCrea and Randolph Scott, ride together, ruminating over times that used to be. Always in the minds of a Westerns-conscious audience is a double-take notion—they could so easily be chewing the fat over Westerns that used to be. They made so many over the years, and they had long been personal friends. It was the happiest inspiration that got them together for this afterglow ride that resulted in two unforgettable performances. But one wonders exactly how they savour the situation—that after so much riding, over so many years, it has taken a late, almost afterthought ride, to place them securely among Western immortals.

The ageing pair, once quick-drawing tamers of the West, have reached a stage of comparative neglect and degradation, when a mission more in the old style presents itself. Steve Judd (McCrea) is asked by a banker to protect the proceeds from a High Sierras gold strike. Judd picks his old buddy Gil Westrum (Scott), now a carnival sharp shooter, as his assistant. Later he also picks a youngster, talented with a gun (Ronald Starr), and it isn't long before the two 'helpers' cook up

their own project. They'll 'secure' the gold for themselves.

There's a conflict, then, between objects and motives of the two old-timers. The Scott character, a realist, has compromised with the shoddy, gimcrack world of his autumnal years, as represented by the Carnival. But the McCrea character has hung on to his pride. Intrinsically a man of moral rectitude, he believes in fulfilling his obligations, 'doing the job'—just like in his old days as lawman.

En route to the mining camp of Coarse Gold what seems to be a cut and dried hi-jacking issue is complicated by other elements. They meet up with a girl (Elsa Knudsen) whose father (R. G. Armstrong) is an almost Biblical character. But despite or because of this background, the girl has nevertheless got herself involved with Billy, scion of one of the wildest families in these wild parts.

Moreover, they find that the *real* profits being made at Coarse Gold seem rather to come from the local whorehouse. So Judd has even been cheated in this respect. Thereafter it's a tale of the trio's involvement with the wild family, who seek revenge when the girl, disillusioned with her marriage to Billy, falls in love with the Ronald Starr character.

Scott and Starr make an unsuccessful attempt at hi-jacking after which Scott seemingly turns his back on the whole scene. So when McCrea is beset by the wild ones it seems he must fight without the aid of his old comrade-in-arms.

Not so, however. The ties of old friendship prove too strong. Scott rides down to join him and they fight the good fight . . . the last one, as it turns out for McCrea. No matter—he dies as he has always tried to live, true to his code.

The basic theme is strong, moving and valid, but, above all, it is the elegiac feel that makes this such a memorable film—the ruminations of the veterans about 'how it was' in the dear departed days, and those oft remarked significant details. These are men with tired feet—they probably also have varicose veins—and how can they be looked upon as glamorous when one views them last thing in long, grubby combinations? And the whores— they really belong in time and place. No prettified Hollywood harlots here.

Joel McCrea and Randolph Scott as two old-timers who take the trail once more in Sam Peckinpah's Ride the High Country *(MGM 1962).*

Peckinpah has also managed to convey the scrubby look of half-tamed country, not quite one thing or the other; territory caught undecided, as it were, at the turn of the times. The whole thing has utter unity of style, the prime essential of a work of art.

Peckinpah's *The Wild Bunch* flaunts our description of 'last desperate fling'. Initially pummelled by critics for its violence—slow motion death and so on—it has now won through to the high reputation that it always deserved. It's a film that excels at many levels. At the deepest it's a profound tragic statement—one of the most serious and sombre made in all movies.

The violent happenings in *The Wild Bunch*, or rather the way in which the camera dwells and plays its tricks upon them, are not so much a matter of relish as an accurate recording of a hard fact— that there's no violence like really desperate violence. And the people here are desperate beyond the limits.

This is the old-time outlaw positively making his last stand, knowing full well it's the last. Time has said—it's 1914—that he's had his day. All, really, that remains for him is to depart in the style to which he's been accustomed—that is, violently.

Desperation and death-wish seem to ride side by side in this picture. If the Bunch (William Holden, Ernest Borgnine, Warren Oates, Ben Johnson, Jaime Sanchez and veteran outlaw hanger-on Edmond O'Brien) are desperate, their

Death and little glory. Sam Peckinpah's typical realistic treatment in scenes from The Wild Bunch *(WB/Seven Arts 1969).*

bounty-hunter pursuers are no less so.

This pack of jackals is led by Robert Ryan, formerly a member of the Bunch. Ryan, whose lined face is as experienced-ravaged as Holden's, has been let out of jail to hunt him down. Either he gets Holden or he goes back inside. Most of his band—his 'trash' as he calls them—have similar dubious inducements.

The pursuit takes the story into Mexico and involves the hi-jacking of armaments by the Bunch from an American supply train (this venture is magnificently shot by Peckinpah) and their delivery to a Mexican general-cum-bandit (Emilio Fernandez).

It is the double-dealing of this villain—evil suppurates from his every pore—that leads to the end of the Bunch in one of the bloodiest screen battles of all time. That and the fact that when the chips are down loyalty to one of the members of the group, Jaime Sanchez, overrides mere love of gold.

Holden's group was never easy to handle. There is conflict and tension among them. They range from the more idealistic Mexican member, Jaime Sanchez, to the wild Gorch brothers, Warren Oates and Ben Johnson. But what binds them together in the last resort is their life-style and its demanding loyalty. Holden puts it this way: 'When you side with a man you stay with him—and if you can't do that you're like some animal.'

But he can read the writing on the wall . . . 'That railroad (source of outlaw livelihood) ain't getting easier . . . it's time we started thinking beyond our guns.' And if the sorry outcome is inevitable . . . 'I wouldn't want it any other way.' Borgnine, his henchman, reflects upon it and then echoes: 'I wouldn't want it any other way, either.'

If it's the end of the road it sees them still together. This seems to be the tenor of it—the exultance and release—with which they face extinction. And when bounty hunter Ryan arrives on the scene of carnage and sees what Mexicans and wild ones have done to each other, and how the buzzards love it, he salutes this spirit, for past loyalties pull at him hard. Amid the last pale valedictory landscape shots they tug him back, in fact, to the old life.

Not only the end of a life-style but the end of an epoch. Never over-stated but always conveyed, this is what gives *The Wild Bunch* its peculiarly elegiac quality. The whole of a brilliant cast seems dipped in it. William Holden's Pike Bishop and Robert Ryan's Deke Thornton are imperishable Western portraits.

Violence seems a matter of spontaneous combustion in this film—the start saw a march of Temperance workers viciously caught in the unheeding crossfire of Bunch and pursuers—but the lulls, in their way, are equally telling; Mexico, its music, life in the villages, the feel of fiesta even on the fringe of violence, the keen look at the Mexican face, especially the faces of the children, sometimes observers, sometimes participating in the whole twisted ethic of violence.

ABOVE *and* BELOW *Scenes from William A. Fraker's* Monte Walsh *(Cinema Center Films 1970), starring Lee Marvin and Jack Palance.*
ABOVE RIGHT *Sam Peckinpah directing David Warner in* The Ballad of Cable Hogue *(WB 1970).*

William A. Fraker's *Monte Walsh* (1970) is another bit of autumn. Here commemorated is the end of the cattle boom, and its key personality. Nothing in terms of Westerns can be sadder than that.

Blessed with the best of beginnings, a novel by Jack Schaefer, who gave a similar sound basis for *Shane*, this moody, impressive picture is a requiem for the cowboy. The cowboy redundant and looking for a shop-keeping job; big business moving in from the East to rationalize; a cowtown with an air of incipient ghost town. Any cowhand worth his coffee and beans could be forgiven for nurturing the thought: far better to go out in gun-blaze like the Wild Bunch.

There are violent happenings in *Monte Walsh*, which had Arizona locations, but not violent-spectacular. Subdued melancholy drapes them as it does everything else.

Two grizzled characters, Lee Marvin and Jack Palance, who have both known better cow-punching times, ride into Harmony, another distant relative of the town portrayed in *Shane*, and think themselves lucky to get jobs on a now Eastern-owned ranch. Among the bunk-house boys is Mitch Ryan, who is glimpsed early on trying to break in a wild grey stallion. The rheumy eye of Marvin still takes expert note.

Relaxation for the two veterans consists of a saloon-gal for Marvin (Jeanne Moreau, making both her U.S. and Western debut) and a widow with a hardware store (Allyn Ann Mclerie) for Palance, who ultimately opts out of ranching for marriage and ironmongering.

The action involves Ryan's unknowing implication in outlawry, his shooting of Palance and Marvin's revenge for his old pal's killing.

But what's left for the old cowhand? Nothing really. His gal has taken ill and died. His friend is dead. He has avenged his death in a reluctant sort of showdown. All his mind can pin on is that he'd managed to master the wild grey stallion in a rumbustious bit of breaking.

Sam Peckinpah's *The Ballad of Cable Hogue*, although still very much concerned with the sere and yellow, offers light, or, at least, lighter relief. At the same time one has to add that there is nothing intrinsically amusing in the fact that the main character, another superannuated type—this time a prospector—meets his death, not by rattlesnake, bullet or thirst but under the wheels of the new-fangled motor car.

Thirst does very much play a part in his history at the outset. Robbed and abandoned by his

partners (Strother Martin and L. O. Jones) in the desert, Jason Robards is saved from certain death by finding water from a spring. And out of this discovery comes a sort of success story. The spring is handy to the stagecoach route and so, assisted by a banker in the nearby dump of a town (Deaddog is the indicative name), he sets up a 'halt' on the trail. In Deaddog he also chums up with the local whore (Stella Stevens). And always aiding and abetting him is a rogue preacher (David Warner) who is ever willing and able to give more than spiritual comfort to the female members of his flock.

The old fellow's project prospers; the sympathetic prostitute pays him a fleeting but rewarding visit; he eventually gets revenge on one of the pardners who left him to die. And the happiest ending seems to purr into view in the form of a splendid car carrying the good-time gal who has finally decided to settle down with him.

But then, as we know, the car has the last grim word on the old Westerner.

Allegory? Or straight romantic comedy? One is never sure but it's a warm and vivid film with a distinctive flavour that teases the palate. Whether the style is peak Peckinpah is another matter.

There is nothing truly elegiac in George Roy Hill's *Butch Cassidy and the Sundance Kid* (1969), although the omens are right.

The time is the turn of the century and the story concerns two real-life outlaws, Robert LeRoy Parker, alias 'Butch Cassidy', born in Utah in 1866, and Harry Longabaugh, alias 'The Sundance Kid', born in Wyoming in 1859.

They were the leaders, with Kentucky-born Harvey Logan, alias 'Kid Currie' (Logan is also featured in the film), of a thinly-knit gang called

the Wild Bunch (nothing to do with Peckinpah's mob), on the loose in Utah, Wyoming, Montana and Idaho, before Butch and Sundance went to try their luck in South America.

Officially they were killed, as in the film, in a tremendous gun battle in Bolivia, but new evidence suggests that two other Americans died there, and the famous pair returned to live quietly in the States. Legend says that Currie took his own life when capture was imminent after a train robbery but, again, this is a matter of doubt. It is possible that he also went to South America. It was a logical step for the 'afterglow' outlaw, chivvied unmercifully on his home ground.

So there is firm foundation for the film, more so than in most Western movies, allowing for the usual uncertainties that shroud the life stories of Western characters.

But anyone looking for a significant rendering of the Butch and Sundance saga will look in vain. It isn't played that way at all.

It has its excitements and it boasts the fashionable climactic bloodbath, but mostly it's played for fun. It's a highly individual Western; a triumph of style, in fact. The style is trendy, witty, oozing with charm; the incessant banter, and Newman urban-hatted on a bike, and the contemporarily lyrical Bacharach pop tune. It's a style that flowers in the Newman-Redford relationship, which is one of the most affecting in movies.

All this gives it the feel and look of fanciful myth carried to a point unusually removed from reality. Backgrounds are sketched rather than etched. You are never really Western in time and place. With belief suspended, feelings are only lightly involved.

But it's derring do at its most flamboyant and given a tangy taste by its essentially modern sense of humour. When Butch and Sundance ride back from relaxation to their Hole-in-the-Wall lair and find they have a mutiny on their hands—Harvey Logan (Ted Cassidy) wants to take over—Butch doesn't quell it with bullets but with a boot up Logan's backside. It's that kind of picture.

Similarly, when too much dynamite scatters the haul from a rail hold-up, this is a moment for wry, amusing comment. And when the posse pursues the pair this is one posse that 'heroes' can't easily shake off. It's always there, cleverly made more irksome by long-shot, so that finally only a 'death defying leap' as the circuses say, can separate hunted from hunters.

Butch Cassidy and the Sundance Kid is undoubtedly a captivating tour de force. Its flavour is preserved from cloying by just the right edge of

wistfulness provided by Katherine Ross as the schoolmarm girl-friend who goes along and who suggests the transience of it all.

Another kind of relationship has made the reputation of Delmer Daves' film *3.10 To Yuma*— one of those movies which, although traditionally based, has its own intense preoccupations. It echoes *High Noon* in some respects, but to harp on the similarity misses the point of a very fascinating picture. *3.10 To Yuma* is fundamentally a subtle psychological drama played out in the claustrophobic setting of a hotel under mental and physical siege. It could be argued that another type of picture could have staged it just as well although the Western form suits it admirably.

Two entirely opposing characters are locked together in conditions of the utmost suspense. The camera plays on their every interaction. Glenn Ford, a free-wheeling outlaw, has lingered too long and typically in amorous dalliance after a crime and has been captured. But how to hold him? For his gang, who have made their getaway, will most likely be back to claim him. Ford is sure of this, as his insouciant bearing makes plain. The cowed citizenry (echoes of the Zinneman picture) become equally certain. Someone has got to get him out of local circulation and then on to a train to Yuma where he can stand trial.

LEFT *Paul Newman, Robert Redford and Katharine Ross, the all-action trio of* Butch Cassidy and the Sundance Kid *(Campanile/20th Century Fox/Newman-Foreman 1969), seen here in still life.*
BELOW *Van Heflin and Glenn Ford in a classic Western suspense film* 3.10 to Yuma *(Columbia 1957).*

Yul Brynner and Steve McQueen in one of the most famous opening scenes of all movies—their Boot Hill ride in John Sturges' The Magnificent Seven *(Mirisch-Alpha 1960).* RIGHT *Another high, wide and handsome scene from* The Magnificent Seven *(Mirisch-Alpha 1960).*

Who will volunteer? There's one applicant and he's motivated by the severest desperation. Struggling farmer Van Heflin sees in the 200 dollars offered for the job his last chance of salvation. His livelihood in peril because of drought, he sees no other way out.

So Ford is spirited away and the hope is that the gang won't trace his whereabouts. Of course, they do. Richard Jaeckel—'the man who slept on the sofa' was how everyone remembered him in this picture—is sinister evidence of discovery.

In a hotel room, therefore, they sweat it out. Van Heflin does most of the sweating, trying to cope, until the train is due, with a situation beyond his experience. For Van Heflin is not even a true professional, as Will Kane was in *High Noon* (who had somewhat similar train-waiting problems), but an amateur, having to deal with Ford's every physical and psychological ruse; having, in the last resort—finding some sort of moral obligation in the job—to resist temptation.

The outlaw, an intelligent man, continually seeks for a chink that will give him his freedom, but becomes deeply fascinated by his 'keeper'. What kind of creature is this who toils on some wretched bit of land, cares so deeply for it, gets no fun at all out of life (by the Ford standards) and seems so densely incorruptible? Is he man or ox?

Whatever he is, he's the complete antithesis of Ford. You get the impression that the outlaw is confronted by a being from another planet. Who wouldn't be intrigued?

The 'soft' ending to this fine film, when at last it gets outside and moves towards the gang and the railway station, has puzzled many critics. It has to be said that Ford's ultimate action doesn't tie in psychologically with the character he has so brilliantly established. After all, psychology is everything in this picture.

Van Heflin could so easily have repeated his patient sod-busting farmer in *Shane*, but, in fact, he adds another layer to him. Ford, in one of his best performances, and he has given many, gets the utmost from his greatest gift—devious and almost forgiveable menace behind the easy charm. The women in the picture, Felicia Farr and Leorna Dana, make a solid contribution to its depth.

The intense preoccupations of director Anthony Mann have already been remarked upon—the passions of his people. His settings are impeccably Western but it's a highly personal world that invites attention.

Man of the West rates as an outstanding example. Violent, sometimes sadistic, it is nonetheless a powerful piece of work in which these elements have their place. They are valid within the framework of double-edged family connections and the ever-intensifying urge of a man to purge the evil in such connections.

Gary Cooper, in the Arizona of the 1870s, sets forth from his little town with six hundred dollars to hire for it a teacher. A trip on a train introduces him to a comely saloon singer (Julie London) but also to a bit of his past he'd rather forget. For when the train is held up it is all too soon apparent that the gang is one to which he'd belonged in the bad old days, led by a villainous kinsman (Lee J. Cobb) and containing another member of the family (John Dehner).

The reformed Cooper's only chance of a getaway —and the girl's chance too—lies in him convincing Cobb and Co., that his loyalties lie with them. Fine, says Cobb, in effect, but do something to prove it.

The 'something' is joining in a stage bank hold-up. . . .

The clash of family loyalties soon makes itself felt. The old man brought him up when he was a boy—the old man still obviously thinks something of him, since he stops an attempt on his life. But the old man is also a villain, and villainy is his prevailing climate and that is why Cooper initially made his breakaway.

The theme is familiar in Mann Westerns and here the mechanics of the 'purging' and the power of it get their best expression.

Nothing seems more unlikely—before viewing— that plot, characters and theme could be borrowed lock, stock and barrel from a Japanese film (a great one at that) and by some bit of Hollywood alchemy be converted into a Western.

But the first few minutes of John Sturges' *The Magnificent Seven* succeeded in convincing almost everyone that the trick had been done. Sturges had Steve McQueen and Yul Brynner riding a hearse up legendary Boot Hill and created a mood of

such mingled braggadocio and peril that audiences began to tingle—and tingle even more in anticipation. It was a triumph of this director's bold, stark style with the camera, and without any qualifications it joins our previously mentioned anthology of great opening sequences. The film didn't quite live up to it—it could hardly be expected to do so—but it was, and remains, a richly enjoyable Western.

The impudence and, indeed, the confidence of the 'borrowing' lay in the fact that the source was so distinguished—Kurosawa's superb *The Seven Samurai*, a compelling tale of intimidated and impoverished mediaeval villagers hiring mercenary warriors to fend off bandit depredations. For samurai read gunfighters, and the Western transference is immediately plausible. In some ways the warriors are like figures from an old morality tale— each has an outstanding face-up characteristic, if not virtue or vice. At the lowest, or facetious level, they are as well defined as the dwarfs in *Snow White*. At least, that remains one admirer's impression.

The villagers in this case are Mexicans, plagued beyond all bearing by the activities of bandit Eli Wallach. Three of them cross the border to offer meagre pay and sustenance for any professionally skilled fighting men who will aid them. About the nucleus of Brynner and McQueen is built a team composed also of James Coburn (he's particularly

ABOVE *Jimmy Stewart casts a wary eye on Marlene Dietrich in* Destry Rides Again
(Universal 1939).
Two scenes from Burt Kennedy's The Good Guys and The Bad Guys *(Ronden 1969).*
*A 'freight load' of feminine charm (*right*) and Robert Mitchum and George Kennedy by the*
*wrecked train (*overleaf*).*

good with a knife), Brad Dexter, Charles Bronson
(he's got a bit of Mexican in him), Robert Vaughan
and latecomer Horst Bucholz, who represents
youth, eagerness and the urge to be proved and
sorted out from the boys.

They have trouble, of course, with the cowed
citizens (no less cowed because they wear som-
breros instead of Derbys), who don't like the all-
out war implications of the Seven's tangle with
Wallach. All, however, is resolved successfully.
But with depletions to the band of heroes. The
villagers especially mourn Bronson. Tough though
he was, he was the one who always had a soft spot
for the children.

The Magnificent Seven was one of those rarities
—an excellent film which also had box-office
written all over it. It was the second biggest
money-maker in Britain in 1961 and it made
household names of Steve McQueen, Charles
Bronson and James Coburn. It did the same for
Horst Bucholz in America—he was already known
in Britain.

Comedy in Westerns, the conscious kind—not
the other sort which can be hilarious in a really bad
oater—seems to come off best when it is firmly
rooted in tradition and classic situation. Apart from

the offshoot touches, as with John Ford at his best,
there are films which manage to contain a whole
basis of comedy, within a framework of exciting
plot development.

Outright 'send-up' Westerns can be dismissed.
They are only successful in odd flashes, such as the
brilliant surrealist bit of nonsense in the 'fuelling
the train with the train' sequence in the Marx
Brothers' film *Go West* (1940).

It is true that there are parody elements in
George Marshall's delightful *Destry Rides Again*
(1939) but the real humour lies not so much in
these sorts of antics, nor the heavily laid on
enquiries of Marlene Dietrich as to the tastes of the
backroom boys, but rather in Jimmy Stewart's
no-gun Destry characterization.

This springs from the same source as Ford's
'characters', recognizable frontier independent-
minded eccentrics, with a firm footing in American
literature, vouchsafed for by such as Mark Twain;
characters often with a roundabout way of making
a point, or pointing a moral, as with Destry's habit
of prefacing each little cautionary parable with:
'I knew a fellow once who . . .' A habit that
inevitably drew the aggrieved riposte: 'You know
too many fellows, Destry . . .'

LEFT *A bicycle made for charm. Paul Newman, Katharine Ross and the machine that added so much to the style of* Butch Cassidy and the Sundance Kid *(Campanile/20th Century Fox/Newman-Foreman 1969).*
RIGHT *Another famous Western fight scene. Mickey Shaughnessy at work in George Marshall's* The Sheepman *(Edmund Grainger 1958).*

The other 'characters' in this film have more than a tinge or two of parody—Mischa Auer's improbable Slavonic cowboy, Charles Winninger's town drunk, and Samuel S. Hinds' nicely played mayor (surely Damon Runyon's Big Falseface in a Western setting).

In retrospect, it's odd how much this movie gains from its rather touching little postscript. Stewart, the unconventional lawman, having pacified his cowtown, strolls the streets with a hero-worshipping lad at his heels, and yet also takes a little cloud of sadness along with him.

With a touch like that in mind it was no real surprise when Marshall came up almost 20 years later with *The Sheepman* (1958) (shot in Montrose, California, and in the San Juan range of the Colorado Rockies), which made very little impact except among the truly discerning, but now ranks with many as the best Western comedy of all time.

This is using the word 'comedy' in the classical, theatrical sense—not in terms of spoofy fun and games, but humour arising from character and situation.

The Sheepman, in fact, is a most exciting picture, solidly based on one of the fiercest Western issues, although it has received comparatively scant attention; the bitter animosity prevailing between cattlemen and sheepmen. So furious was the feuding that it often exploded into a malevolence that was a blot on the name of 'cowboy'—involving the murder of sheep and shepherds alike. Wyoming and Arizona both experienced the nastier manifestations.

Sheep and cattle don't mix—this is reckoned to be an agricultural truism the world over—and so when Glenn Ford arrives in cattle territory, cheerfully proclaiming that he's bringing in sheep, all is set for a full-scale feuding.

But there's something incongruous in the sight of sheep in the Western movie setting—especially when there's a hard man in charge of them. By the standards of cattlemen sheep-herding is unmanly, more unworthy even than sod-busting. And so the comedy element is built in—the disgust of the cattlemen at the mere sight of sheep, only equalled by disgust at the sight of Ford, tending them, entirely unabashed.

Marshall handles it all beautifully and is well served by first rate comedy talent—Ford (again the steel behind the smile, but an easier smile); Shirley Maclaine, many people's favourite comedienne, in marvellous form; Edgar Buchanan, as a devious freewheeling old-timer; Mickey Shaughnessy, as Jumbo the lumbering town tough; Pedro Gonzales-Gonzales, the much ponched, sombreroed and lugubrious-looking herdsman.

It's a great mixture, nicely stirred—not forgetting the 'straight man' cattleman, Leslie Nielsen.

Henry Hathaway's *True Grit* can stand up very well as Western adventure on its own account —the story of a young girl (Kim Darby) hiring an old lawman (John Wayne) to seek out the murderer (Jeff Corey) of her father. Texas Ranger Glen Campbell rides along in the hope of collecting reward money.

Suspense, action—the film has more than its share—and the practised hand of Hathaway sees that justice is done in these terms. But when this has faded, when perhaps even the engaging and forceful Miss Darby has dwindled in time, Duke Wayne's portrait of that fat, mean, greedy, eye-patched, whisky sozzling and yet in some strange way lovable lawman will remain.

It will remain as a fine comedy performance, not as self-parody of his many Western roles, as has been rather ungraciously suggested. Marshal Rooster Cogburn is a kind of Western Falstaff with a cutting edge. Without any doubt the West knew characters like him. John Ford would know exactly what Wayne was about in this role. Even when Wayne got an Oscar for this performance it was said that the award was *really* for long service.

ABOVE *John Wayne and Kim Darby in* True Grit *(Paramount 1969).*
BELOW *and* OPPOSITE *Three scenes from the zany* Cat Ballou *(Hecht Corp. 1965), starring Jane Fonda and Lee Marvin.*

When he says in the declining moments of this picture: 'Come and see a fat old man some time,' that's a standing invitation. Audiences will want a peek at this portrait for some considerable time to come.

A salute also to some rewarding moments in Elliot Silverstein's *Cat Ballou* (1965) and another Oscar-winning performance. This time it's from Lee Marvin in the double role of boozy, played-out gunfighter and opposing badman brother. Jane Fonda is the gal who heads an all-male gang out to avenge her father's murder.

The Western says it with music.
ABOVE Oklahoma *(R. & H. Pictures 1955).*
ABOVE RIGHT Seven Brides for Seven Brothers *(MGM 1954).*
BELOW RIGHT Calamity Jane *(WB 1953).*

What about the Western set to music? 'Never!' say the ultra-purists. For the benefit of mainstream Western fans let's put it this way. If in our celestial Festival of all-time-greats we feel the need for intermission (perhaps musical intermission) to get rid, say, of the taste of dust after *Red River*, or calm down the pulse-rate after the agonies of *The Wild Bunch*, where would fancy fall?

Perhaps it would fall on Zinneman's *Oklahoma* (1955) with Howard Keel revelling in a beautiful morning and Rod Steiger making that extraordinary black-hearted cowhand contribution? Or David Butler's *Calamity Jane* (1953), with Howard Keel again, playing Wild Bill Hickok, and Doris Day giving her celebrated all-stops-out impression of Martha Jane Cannaray, complete with tribute to the Deadwood Stage?

Or on Lee Marvin's and Clint Eastwood's broad-minded marital arrangements in Joshua Logan's *Paint Your Wagon* (1969)?

A last pause for re-consideration. Let's not forget that Oregon spells early Western settlement and though at times it seems that it's set in some truly rural northern never-never land, the location of Stanley Donen's *Seven Brides for Seven Brothers* (1954) was, in fact, placed firmly in Oregon. Presumably the seven brothers with marital requirements no less pressing than Marvin and Eastwood trekked up the Oregon Trail from Independence, Missouri and are therefore legal emigrants in our Western fold.

One hopes so, profoundly, for this lovable tale of primitive brethren, although not in Rome, doing what the Romans did when short of female company, is often pure enchantment. With Howard Keel, once more, and Jane Powell and the inspired choreography of Michael Kidd, it's a feast in itself for any movie festival.

Whither the Western?

ALL the world loves a Western. A merry tinkling in box-offices throughout the planet has long testified to the fact. It's an entertainment form that is universally acceptable. It attracts and communicates whatever the local language. Deep down there must be something common to all men in what concerns a Western movie.

It might well be that the common factor is a subconscious rejection of the computerized blueprint that is being prepared for all of us—whatever the language. (Things were simpler on the 'wide prairee'.) Or cynics might say that there is no need to look further for a reason beyond the theory that the biggest audience in the world is composed of men who are incurably boys at heart.

The world, anyway, acknowledges its affection and the strangest tribute it has paid is to try and take the whole thing over. If imitation is, indeed, the sincerest form of flattery, America should be gratified.

There is nothing new in the copy-Western. European producers have toyed with it over the years, recognizing the box-office potential and seeking to cash in. What is new is the vast effort and the commercial success that has attended these copyist activities over the last decade.

The Germans led the way in this sixties phenomenon with a sort of Teutonic Western all their own. Their source was a writer named Karl May who was born in 1842 and who, without trekking any

BELOW *and* LEFT *Kenneth More goes West in* The Sheriff of Fractured Jaw *(20th Century Fox 1958).*

ABOVE *A disapproving Eastern eye on the West from Kenneth More in* The Sheriff of Fractured Jaw *(20th Century Fox 1958).*
OPPOSITE *Two scenes from 'Spaghetti Westerns',* A Fistful of Dollars *(Jolly Film/Constantin/Ocean 1964) and* The Good, The Bad and The Ugly *(Produzioni Europee Associate 1966), in which Clint Eastwood (below) had the company of Lee Van Cleef and Eli Wallach.*

farther west than East Germany, somehow established himself as an authority on Western America. The main character in his books was Old Shatterhand, a kind of compendium of imagined frontier virtues, skills and characteristics. His redskin counterpart was the noble Winnetou the Warrior.

Films based on the May characters became big business in Germany. To the eye of the Western connoisseur they are laughable. Stars more familiar to British and American audiences, such as Lex Barker and Stewart Granger, played in them, but this didn't help. Naïve, awkwardly synthetic, they are an oddity—odder even than the Singing Cowboy productions. At times they tend rather to give the impression of a No. 2 touring company, lost and so far from home that they've really forgotten what it's all about and aren't even certain that they've rummaged in the right wardrobe.

More to the point, certainly in terms of impact, were the Italian productions and co-productions—there was a kind of Common Market zeal for co-operation in these films—that were to earn the dubious label of Spaghetti Westerns. They were based on the sound financial premise that it was cheap to make Westerns in rugged European locations such as offered by Spain and Yugoslavia.

It is only fair to add that American producers had already realized this. The British, in fact, could claim to be trail-blazers with *The Sheriff of Fractured Jaw* (1958), which was a somewhat tepid attempt at a comedy Western, starring Jayne Mansfield and Kenneth More, and shot in Spain.

The Italians, realistically, invested more heavily than the Germans in genuine American Western talent. Fortunes, financial and otherwise, were sometimes made and raised by these emigrant Western actors.

The outstanding example was Clint Eastwood...

Eastwood was in at the outset of the Spaghetti trend. A recognized star in 30 countries of television Westerns, after almost ten years in the popular *Rawhide* he had the urge to get back into movies and so took the first available opportunity, an Italian Western to be shot in Spain and directed by Sergio Leone.

From what Eastwood has said about this venture it seems to have had him in two minds at the start. It seems that the production had money problems and there were firework shows of Latin temperament. At one time he was almost back at the airport seeking a quick flight home.

But he stayed on in a scene of not a little confusion. Spanish and Italian verbs spattered all around him—it must be remembered that these were the early days—and without doubt he is now profoundly thankful that he saw it all through.

For this particular hybrid of an oater, with Clint playing an unnamed, ponchoed professional killer, was none other than *A Fistful of Dollars* (1964). It

wasn't too long before this production had grossed over five million dollars. The whole thing must have made the Japanese furious, for once again one of their samurai tales had been as good as filched. First there had been the case of *The Seven Samurai* —now it was another Kurosawa film, *Yojimbo*. The Japanese, incidentally, also went through a period of producing Westerns, but they always showed a marked deference for the real thing. For instance, they would never plot their stories north of the Mexican border.

Leone and Eastwood spread their conquests further with *For A Few Dollars More* (1967) and *The Good, The Bad And The Ugly* (1968). The success of the Dollars films, as they came to be known, was extraordinary. It knew no boundaries. If ever there was a case of 'coals to Newcastle' it was with these films, for the American public flocked to them, too.

'*Spaghetti Style*'—*four typical scenes.*
LEFT For a Few Dollars More
*(Produzioni Europee Associate/Arturo
Gonzales/Constantin 1965).*
RIGHT The Good, The Bad and The
Ugly *(Produzioni Europee Associate
1966).*
BELOW *Two scenes from* A Fistful
of Dollars *(Jolly Film/Constantin/
Ocean 1964).*

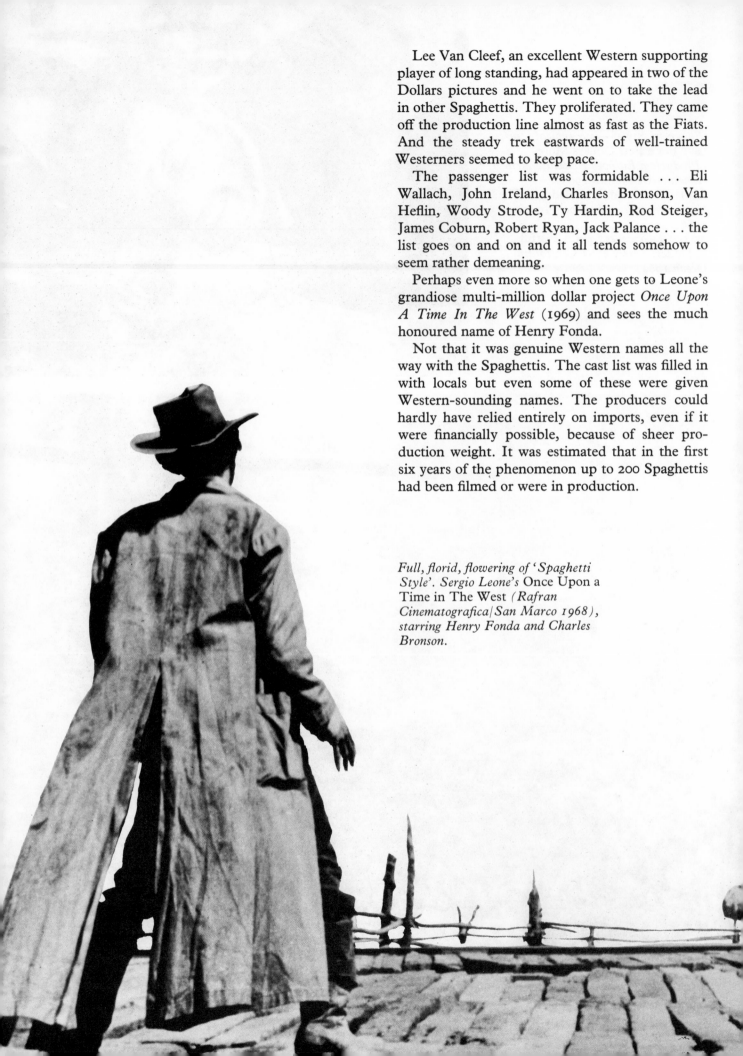

Lee Van Cleef, an excellent Western supporting player of long standing, had appeared in two of the Dollars pictures and he went on to take the lead in other Spaghettis. They proliferated. They came off the production line almost as fast as the Fiats. And the steady trek eastwards of well-trained Westerners seemed to keep pace.

The passenger list was formidable ... Eli Wallach, John Ireland, Charles Bronson, Van Heflin, Woody Strode, Ty Hardin, Rod Steiger, James Coburn, Robert Ryan, Jack Palance ... the list goes on and on and it all tends somehow to seem rather demeaning.

Perhaps even more so when one gets to Leone's grandiose multi-million dollar project *Once Upon A Time In The West* (1969) and sees the much honoured name of Henry Fonda.

Not that it was genuine Western names all the way with the Spaghettis. The cast list was filled in with locals but even some of these were given Western-sounding names. The producers could hardly have relied entirely on imports, even if it were financially possible, because of sheer production weight. It was estimated that in the first six years of the phenomenon up to 200 Spaghettis had been filmed or were in production.

Full, florid, flowering of 'Spaghetti Style'. Sergio Leone's Once Upon a Time in The West *(Rafran Cinematografica/San Marco 1968), starring Henry Fonda and Charles Bronson.*

Artistic merits aside—where you would have to look hard to find them—it wasn't a particularly pleasant film that was being produced. At one time the Italian Minister of Tourism deplored the questionable taste of the Spaghettis, and one could well understand his alarm, for the part played in the world cinema by the Italian industry has mainly been a revered and honourable one.

It wasn't just a matter of violence in the Italian Western. Violence is endemic in Westerns. It was rather that violence had consciously degenerated into downright sadism and the flavour throughout was mean, nasty and ugly.

The ultimate twist to the tale came when Hollywood produced its own Italian-style Western, *Hang 'Em High* (1968). This film was built around Eastwood, the man who really by chance—by just wanting to get back into movies—had played such a major part in the start of it all.

It's possible that the Western may find new trails, but the Italian Spaghetti isn't one of them. It's a cul-de-sac and a tedious and unsavoury one at that. It's just another return to what has always been basic about the Western film—the conveyor-belt, cash-in role.

A phenomenon most certainly but an irrelevance in the context of distinguished Western movies.

For borrowing the mechanics can never be enough. The Western at its best—to return to our initial argument—is one nation's history, illumined by its own nationals.

It's rooted in feeling—not in the mechanics of action—although action, of course, has a predominant part in it, for they were active times. The feeling may be ebullient, as with early Ford, reflecting the belief that a new country, a brighter future is being created and that an old skin of sad experience is being sloughed off. Or it may be bitter, as with later Ford, or angry-elegiac (Peckinpah) in the sense that the new experience was wasted or the dream was unfulfilled. But it is essential that the experience is yours by birthright in order to express it fully, and this is why the Western is not really for export.

There are other reasons—there's the matter of style, for instance. Speech rhythms that put flesh on the bones of a script, the way a Westerner walked (still does), the way he looked right and as natural as sunlight in outlandish kinds of clothes. A corollary is our past experience of Americans in European costume dramas. These seldom worked.

Obliquely, Peter Bogdanovich's magnificent *The Last Picture Show* (1972) is more of a Western —though it would never put in a claim for this—

Clint Eastwood starred in Hang 'em High *(Freeman/Malpaso 1967), a Hollywood Western that seemed to take its cue from the Italian style.*

than anything that comes off the foreign production lines. The 'feel' of it, the memory, is there. Set in a small Texan town of the 1950s it's a film that's imbued with the sadness of a lost dream, and the dream, by inference, is the West. There is a significant moment in this film—it's been noted before but it bears repeating—when up on the screen there's a shot of another screen framing John Wayne and co., booted and spurred and all rarin' to go.

The little picture-house is closing down and the last movie they're showing there is Hawks' *Red River*. The audience—what's left of them—watch Wayne and his drovers rein their horses flamboyantly before heading north. It's a moment of big bold gestures, spelling out vigour, confidence and the 'start of something big'. It's the start, in fact, of the building of a cattle empire, part of the dream.

But the Western dream has finished up as this spiritual ghost town, impoverished of everything that set the wheels in motion not so very long before. Soon the heirs of it all won't even be able to watch a Western in its rightful home. Even the rituals attending the watching of a Western, the popcorn and the candy and the love-play in the back seats, are doomed. If there had to be a last one—there's a little mercy here—then *Red River* couldn't be bettered as the final choice. What it all amounts to is a punctuation mark at the end of a time-scale. The whole thing says: 'The dream stops here!'

The Western is by no means a narrow form, but at its best it has to be infused with feeling—feeling about the time and the place and the people and their problems. It's a *particular* kind of film.

But it is also amazingly resilient. It has seen all of the changes that have affected cinema, gained from the ones that have suited it, weathered the others. Sound, colour, the big screen (which always became it), polaroid-spectacled 3-D (remember the oohs! and aahs! as arrows hurtled into the auditorium?), the wide screen, Cinerama—no doubt there will be more and the Western will deal with them. In the view of at least one observer the Western seldom comes off in miniature—another way of saying that it loses out on the T.V. screen.

Where next? Surely the seam must be near exhaustion?

These thoughts have often been pondered in the past, especially in the lean years when other forms of cinema have predominated and nothing of

Western note has come from the studios, or, pessimistically, they have fallen back on some quick-returns cycle such as the 'B' feature.

Experience, however, teaches us that despite the warning notes sounded and the lamentations about better times past that usually attend the passing of each decade, the Western has a built-in ability to renew itself, to do the trick once more, to uncover some fresh nugget that no one had ever thought to put a boot to.

There is infinite variety left in the genre and it is partly this residue of resources, rather than the attractive balletics of a man and a horse, perennially appealing though these may be, that justifies faith in its future. Students of the period will tell you that it still teems with incidents. And as for themes, have they *all* been thoroughly explored?

The Indian. Could anyone fairly say that he's received definitive treatment? Hardly so. Surely the real answer is that his tragedy has only been touched upon. Who's heard of the death of the buffalo save in terms of Buffalo Bill and similar coloured-up hunters, and then only as background to the more romantic phases of their lives.

Yet the extermination of the buffalo—they vanished at the rate of two million a year from 1872 to 1885 according to one estimate—spelt absolute economic disaster to the aboriginal population. True, it would be difficult to film, merely *because* of the death of the buffalo, but something rich as robes could still be wrapped around it.

Was the fight to a death utterly inevitable between redskins and whites? Possibly, in one way or the other. And yet the relationship between Mormon settlers and Indians suggests that it could have been otherwise. One writer of the times, although seemingly no lover of Mormons, stated emphatically that the Latter Day Saints had steered clear of the usual Indian troubles by approaching them as 'brothers and equals without any desire to force civilization upon them. . . .'

What, of course, was happening, was that the red men were dealing with an entirely different sort of society than the basically acquisitive kind they met elsewhere. The Mormons, it has been said, saw them as one of the lost tribes of Israel and as long as they conformed to Mormon teaching, protection was theirs and intermarriage not frowned upon.

Is there something here for a director looking for an unexplored pathway from the main pioneering trail?

RIGHT *Dustin Hoffman in* Little Big Man *(Stockbridge/Hiller 1970).*
Sympathy for the Indians.
OVERLEAF *A blazing scene from Andrew McLaglen's* Cahill *(Batjac 1973).*

LEFT *A scene from the spectacular* Man in The Wilderness *(WB/Wilderness Films 1971), starring Richard Harris.*
ABOVE *Richard Harris again, this time in a Sam Peckinpah Western,* Major Dundee *(Jerry Bresler 1965).*

Then there's the fag-end of the great rumbustious cattle-boom. Not the infiltration of irksome homesteaders, but the logical end of all booms—the busting of, because of changed economic needs and methods. *Monte Walsh* examined the beginnings of the end. Someone could take it from there.

And perhaps someone else might listen to a long plea, couched in typically diffident terms, by the Westerner himself—Gary Cooper.

Cooper looked back, beyond *High Noon* and its tensions, and yearned for films that would get down to the fundamentals of pioneering life, the simplicity of it, with the accent on the grittiness of day to day life and the people who lived it, rather than the more lurid interludes.

And he appealed for more credit to be given to the immigrants, freshly in from overseas, who played a greater role in the pioneering than most films make apparent.

A sort of gritty pastoral with just a little gunplay and a token shower of arrows? Seriously, it deserves a close look.

Themes and story lines apart, there is another reason why a director need not be intimidated by what might seem a top-heavy past.

The Western fan is both understanding and undemanding. He will appreciate a new story-line or theme but he is quite happy to slip into an old one, as into a favourite armchair. What he *does* relish, if he's a discerning filmgoer, is the fresh interpretation.

So in the end it all comes down to the personal vision of the director, fired by a script that excites his own sense of style and particular preoccupations.

To achieve the desired result, as with all forms of art, is a difficult enough task in itself. But the film director has more than a battle with his own talents on his hands. He has to fight a war on several fronts and it is rare that he can claim total victory. Budgetary and studio demands, the vagaries of powerful actors—so much can come between him and the vision. The best that can be hoped for is a kind of compromise.

Sometimes the interference can be well-nigh calamitous. . . .

Sam Pekinpah apparently suffered much because of what was ultimately done to *Major Dundee* (1965), obviously a major work in conception, with enough good things still contained to give a taste of the might-have-been.

Certainly, its starting point was one of the likeliest ever—two officers on opposing sides in the Civil War, Charlton Heston and Richard Harris, becoming reluctant allies in a revenge mission against Apaches. And certainly the characters themselves, so complex, so contrasting, constitute one of the most intense relationships in all Western movies.

But whole scenes were never filmed and bits of others were left on the cutting-room floor, so that the film that was in Peckinpah's mind wasn't the one that was subsequently released. It must have been a traumatic experience for the director who had already given the world the classic *Ride the High Country*.

More and more one tends to look to Peckinpah for good things to come. He has some kind of personal involvement with the form, even perhaps commitment to it, that illumines it in a unique way

and gives it a memorable potency. One would like to see him let loose on the pioneering theme with something original (yes, it's possible) in the way of stories.

It is certain that the throes of settlement would be given a new feeling, the landscape would surprise us, and the settlers themselves would have a different reality.

Reality, in all its gradations, is the key to the secret. Much play is made about a Western 'mythology', meaning that the heroes of the Western film are kinsfolk to godlike heroes of the distant past.

But it's not necessarily so—demigods really only belong in bad 'B' features. Surely if one examines the films one admires the converse is more accurate. Distance lends no enchantment. It is the immediacy that appeals. The events took place within almost living memory. In a relative sense one can say that the people were people of our times. And gods? Never! Grandma can still remember stories told on mother's knee of Great-Aunt Jane who went off by covered wagon to California and *everyone* knew just how silly and frail was little Jane.

No, they are ordinary flesh and blood, raised by time and circumstance to heroic stature. One identifies with them, feels for them. One doesn't identify with gods.

Gary Cooper's Will Kane in *High Noon* is a vulnerable, worried man. Every male in the audience shares his fallibility and is on his side.

One shouldn't sympathize with Gregory Peck as *The Gunfighter* but somehow one does. He's so tired. He wants to sit a while by his own fireside. We all know the feeling.

Similarly with Alan Ladd in *Shane*. Ultimately Ladd is a loser, like many of us. Somewhere along the line he's missed his chance. But he's still excellent at the thing he does well. We all have one

trick of the trade that will never let us down, whatever happens.

Or, to change chairs, at the other side of the sod-buster's table, who hasn't felt like farmer Van Heflin. 'I've slogged and I've slogged and what's to show for it. . . .'

Van Heflin slogging it out again in *3.10 To Yuma*; then poor unbalanced (surely he was unbalanced?) Jack Burns, played by Kirk Douglas in *Lonely are the Brave*.

Even William Holden's Pike Bishop in *The Wild Bunch*. Outlaw he may be, but the man's been made redundant by modernization and he's putting a brave face on it. Again, we know how he feels.

When the next great Western comes stealing upon us, as it assuredly will, most probably unheralded and for a while unsung, these are the kind of people who will claim our allegiance and time and again press their acquaintanceship.

One feels for the hero of the truly great Western, for instance with the desperate Kirk Douglas (above left) in Lonely are the Brave *(Universal-Int./Joel 1955), and with the equally desperate Gregory Peck (left) in* The Gunfighter *(20th Century Fox 1950).*

Bibliography

Acknowledgments

Books consulted include the following which are invaluable further reading for all interested in the subject and period:

A Pictorial History of the Western Film by William K. Everson, Citadel Press, 1969.

A Pictorial History of Westerns by Michael Parkinson and Clyde Jeavons, Hamlyn, 1972.

The Western—An Illustrated Guide by Allen Eyles, A. Zwemmer/A. S. Barnes, 1967.

John Ford by Peter Bogdanovich, Studio Vista, 1967.

Horizons West by Jim Kitses, Thames and Hudson, 1969.

Behind the Screen by Kenneth Macgowan, Delacorte Press, 1965.

The American Cowboy by J. B. Frantz and J. E. Choate, University of Oklahoma Press, 1955. Thames and Hudson, 1956.

The Films of Gary Cooper by Homer Dickens, Citadel Press, 1970.

Massacres of the Mountains by J. F. Dunn, first published in 1886. First British edition, Eyre and Spottiswoode, 1963.

The publishers owe a debt of gratitude to the numerous people and organizations who have helped make this book possible by allowing them the run of their collections of stills and memorabilia and by putting information of one kind or another at their disposal.

The publishers are particularly grateful to the Alan Frank Collection for the provision of stills and invaluable information; to the staff of all departments of the British Film Institute; to Twentieth Century Fox for stills from *The Bravados, Broken Lance, Butch Cassidy and the Sundance Kid, Buffalo Bill, The Ox-Bow Incident, Broken Arrow, The Gunfighter, Rawhide, Jesse James, Frontier Marshal, My Darling Clementine and Warlock;* to John R. Hamilton Globe, Pictorial Press, and to Syndication International.

Finally to all those in the film industry without whom this book would have been impossible, goes a special thank you.

Index of Film Titles

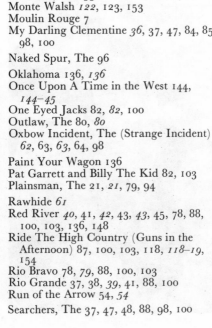

General Index

Planned by Berkeley Publishers Ltd, 20 Wellington Street, London WC2
Designed by Brian Paine
This edition published 1979 *by Galley Press in association with Cathay Books*
59 *Grosvenor Street, London* W1
ISBN 0 904644 88 X
© 1976 *Hennerwood Publications Ltd*
Produced by Mandarin Publishers Limited 22A Westlands Road, Quarry Bay, Hong Kong
Printed in Hong Kong